Bhagavad Gita

Summarized and Simplified

~

A Comprehensive and Easy-to-Read Summary of the Divine Song of God

~

HARI CHETAN

A Gift for You

In the daily commotion that characterizes our lives nowadays, it is quite easy to lose track of oneself. And so it is important for us to maintain our mental equilibrium by connecting with our spiritual selves on a regular basis.

Download Hari Chetan's **free Bhagavad Gita Workbook** designed especially for the readers of his books.

This workbook will help you test your knowledge of the core concepts given in the Bhagavad Gita, and to keep you on track in your spiritual journey.

Try it. It's free to download and is very useful!

Visit **www.harichetan.com** to download.

The Bhagavad Gita Series

Book 1: Bhagavad Gita - The Perfect Philosophy: 15 Reasons That Make the Song of God the Most Scientific Ideology

Book 2: Bhagavad Gita (in English): The Authentic English Translation for Accurate and Unbiased Understanding

Book 3: 30 Days to Understanding the Bhagavad Gita: A Complete, Simple, and Step-by-Step Guide to the Million-Year-Old Confidential Knowledge

Book 4: The Bhagavad Gita Summarized and Simplified: A Comprehensive and Easy-to-Read Summary of the Divine Song of God

Book 5: Mind Management through the Bhagavad Gita: Master your Mindset in 21 Days and Discover Unlimited Happiness and Success

All Books: Bhagavad Gita (In English) – The Complete Collection: 5-Books-in-1

DEDICATED TO

The busy but dedicated seekers
all over the world

Thoughts of Intellectuals on the Bhagavad Gita

"When doubts haunt me, when disappointments stare me in the face, and I see not one ray of hope on the horizon, I turn to Bhagavad Gita and find a verse to comfort me; and I immediately begin to smile in the midst of overwhelming sorrow. Those who meditate on the Gita will derive fresh joy and new meanings from it every day." ~ Mahatma Gandhi

"The marvel of the Bhagavad Gita is its truly beautiful revelation of life's wisdom which enables philosophy to blossom into religion." ~ Hermann Hesse

"(The Bhagavad Gita is) one of the most clear and comprehensive summaries of perennial philosophy ever revealed; hence its enduring value is subject not only to India but to all of humanity." ~ Aldous Huxley

"That the spiritual man need not be a recluse, that union with the divine life may be achieved and maintained in the midst of worldly affairs, that the obstacles to that union lie not outside us but within us — such is the central lesson of the Bhagavad Gita." ~ Annie Besant

"In the morning I bathe my intellect in the stupendous and cosmogonal philosophy of the Bhagavad Gita in comparison with which our modern world and its literature seem puny and trivial." ~ Henry David Thoreau

"I owed a magnificent day to the Bhagavad Gita. It was as if an empire spoke to us, nothing small or unworthy, but large, serene, consistent, the voice of an old intelligence which in another age and climate had pondered and thus disposed of the same questions which exercise us." ~ Ralph Waldo Emerson

"Bhagavad Gita is a true scripture of the human race, a living creation rather than a book, with a new message for every age and a new meaning for every civilization." ~ Sri Aurobindo

"The most beautiful, perhaps the only true philosophical song existing in any known tongue ... perhaps the deepest and loftiest thing the world has to show." ~ Wilhelm von Humboldt

"I am 90% through the Bhagavad Gita ... My inner Arjuna is being channelled." ~ Will Smith

"The Bhagavad Gita deals essentially with the spiritual foundation of human existence. It is a call of action to meet the obligations and duties of life; yet keeping in view the spiritual nature and grander purpose of the universe." ~ Jawaharlal Nehru

"I hesitate not to pronounce the Gita a performance of great originality, of sublimity of conception, reasoning and diction almost unequalled; and a single exception, amongst all the known religions of mankind." ~ Lord Warren Hastings

"Those are spiritual things to reflect upon yourself, life, the world around you and see things the other way. I thought it (the Bhagavad Gita) was quite appropriate." ~ Sunita Williams

"Abandoning all forms of engagements, take refuge in Me alone. I will liberate you from all sins. Do not grieve."

[Lord Krishna to Arjuna - Bhagavad Gita 18.66]

Table of Contents

Introduction

When he enters this world, a living being's mind is blank, except for the recollections of being kept within a cage for several weeks or months. Then his learning process begins gradually. Throughout his life, he keeps learning from various sources — family, teachers, friends, strangers, the environment, nature, books, television, movies, the internet, and whatnot. But there always remains a large knowledge gap that needs to be filled. None of these sources of knowledge gives him an insight into *himself*. At all times, he identifies himself with a face, a gender, an address, a city, and a country. If he obtains a degree and a professional designation, he begins to associate himself with those qualifications and titles. All his life he thinks himself to be the child of his parents, the husband of his wife, the father of his children, and so on. However, that void is never filled, because none of these is his true identity.

Most of us never ask ourselves who we truly are, where we came from and for what, where we will go once we die, and other similar questions about our identity. It's true that at some point in our lives, we all face these questions. However, we have no idea where to find the answers and are too busy to keep looking. So, we don't bother much.

The Bhagavad Gita has all of those answers.

The Bhagavad Gita is a book of open secrets. 'Open' because we all have access to it. 'Secret' because most of us do not care to expose ourselves to that knowledge. And many of those who do enter this magnificent pool of wisdom do not receive much out of it, all because they were expecting a quick fix mantra that would solve all of their problems instantaneously.

The Bhagavad Gita is the comprehensive instruction manual provided by God to us for living a perfect life in this material world.

Even after reading over a hundred books on the subject, I haven't been able to define the Bhagavad Gita in one sentence any better than this. Over the past decade, I've tried to come up with a comprehensive definition of the Bhagavad Gita; but every time I tried, the definition grew into a one-page synopsis. I eventually concluded that the only way to comprehend Gita properly is to read it from beginning to end, or at least a comprehensive synopsis of its teachings that covers all the knowledge it contains.

Before we get into the magnificence of the Bhagavad Gita, let me present a brief historical backdrop of what led to the situation when God

Himself sung His divine song to His devotee for the benefit of all humanity.

A brief history of the Bhagavad Gita

In the ancient Kuru dynasty of Hastinapur, appeared King Shantanu. He had a wife named Ganga. As an after-effect of a curse by Brahma, Ganga had to leave Shantanu. They had a son named Devavrata, who was gifted in every way. Shantanu fell in love with Satyavati, a fisherman's adopted daughter, and wished to marry her. Her father, however, approved of the marriage on the condition that Satyavati's son inherits the Hastinapur crown. When Devavrata learned of this, he gave up his right to the throne and made a vow to never marry and to serve the throne until the end of his days. Devavrata thus earned the name Bhishma (one who has taken a terrible vow).

One of the sons of Shantanu and Satyavati, named Vichitravirya, inherited the throne from his father. He had two wives named Ambika and Ambalika. Ambika gave birth to a son named Dhritarashtra, and Ambalika had a son named Pandu. Because Dhritarashtra was born blind, his stepbrother Pandu, though younger than him, ascended to the throne. Dhritarashtra saw this as an injustice to himself. He married Gandhari and had a hundred sons and one daughter with her. Duryodhana was the eldest of their children. Dhritarashtra had another son with his second wife, Vaishya, named Yuyutsu. Pandu also married twice and had three sons, Yudhisthira, Bhima, and Arjuna, from his first wife Kunti, and two sons, Nakula and Sahadeva, from his second wife Madri.

Pandu died young, and thereafter Dhritarashtra became the king, much to his delight. His sons, called the Kauravas, despised their cousins, the sons of Pandu, known as the Pandavas. When they grew up, the kingdom was divided into two halves, with the fertile half going to the Kauravas and the infertile half going to the Pandavas. The Pandavas, however, used their skills and the help of their cousin Krishna to transform the barren region into a heavenly empire. When Duryodhana visited their kingdom, Indraprastha, he became very envious.

Duryodhana even attempted to kill the five sons of Pandu, as well as Kunti, by burning them alive. But with the help of Krishna, who happened to be Kunti's nephew, the Pandavas and Kunti were able to escape.

Then Duryodhana invited his cousins to a 'friendly' game of gambling. Duryodhana cheated at the game with the help of his uncle Shakuni and took everything from the Pandavas, including Draupadi, their wife. Duryodhana even tried to strip Draupadi in front of everyone. Draupadi, however, was saved by Krishna. Duryodhana ordered that the Pandavas serve thirteen years in the woods including one year in anonymity. The rules were designed in such a way that if the Pandavas were discovered in the final year, they would have to start over.

When the Pandavas returned after the completion of the term and demanded their kingdom back, Duryodhana refused, claiming that they were identified in the final year and so they needed to repeat the thirteen-year sentence.

War remained the only option for the Pandavas. Arjuna, the third of the Pandava brothers and the best archer in the world, and Duryodhana went to see Krishna and ask for his assistance. As fate would have it, they both left at the same time. Duryodhana was the first to arrive. Krishna was sound asleep at the time, and Duryodhana stood by His head, waiting for Him to awaken. Arjuna arrived a few minutes later and, seeing Krishna sleeping, reverently stood by His feet. Because Arjuna was the first person that Krishna saw when He awoke, much to Duryodhana's annoyance, tradition mandated that Krishna accept Arjuna's request first. He declared that one side could have His army and the other could have Him. He, however, made it clear that He would not take part in the upcoming war as a king or warrior. Duryodhana was aware of Krishna's vast military forces and was enraged that Arjuna had been given the choice first. However, he was surprised and delighted when Arjuna chose Krishna over His military troops. Knowing Krishna's true identity, Arjuna was content to have his Lord on his side, regardless of whether He fought or not. He requested Krishna to be his charioteer and guide in the great war, which Krishna pleasantly agreed to.

Dhritarashtra, being blind, could not participate in the war. However, out of concern for his sons, the Kauravas, he wished to know what was going on on the battlefield in real time. Sage Ved Vyasa, an avatar of Lord Vishnu, granted divine eyes to his disciple and Dhritarashtra's charioteer, Sanjaya, so that he could see the happenings of the battle and narrate the same to Dhritarashtra.

All armies assembled on the great battlefield of Kurukshetra. When the war was about to begin, Arjuna asked Krishna to draw up his chariot in between the two vast armies, so that he could see who all had gathered to fight in this great battle. As he surveyed both sides, he saw friends and family all around. Standing opposite him were his cousins, the sons of his uncle, Dhritarashtra. Present also was his military teacher Drona, for whom he has a great deal of respect. The opposing armies were led by Bhishma, the great-grandsire of the Kuru dynasty, who had lavished love on all the Pandava princes, especially Arjuna. Bhishma had to take Duryodhana's side, as he had pledged to remain a servant of the throne all his life. Arjuna then saw many other friends and relatives standing on both sides, ready to fight. Overcome by love and compassion for his loved ones, Arjuna slumped down on his chariot, and perplexed about the right course of action, asked Krishna to be his spiritual guide and to advise him.

Noticing Arjuna's bewilderment, Lord Krishna transformed into his spiritual master and sang to him His divine song, the Bhagavad Gita, enlightening him about the greatest truths in the universe and dispelling all his doubts and fears.

This divine conversation was recorded in writing by Veda Vyasa in the form of 700 verses (or 701 verses, depending on the way the Sanskrit verses are grouped), separated into 18 chapters. The Bhagavad Gita forms chapters 23 to 40 of Book VI of the Mahabharata.

The magic of the Bhagavad Gita

I call the Bhagavad Gita "the end of self-help," completely agreeing with the following words of Henry David Thoreau: "In the morning I bathe my intellect in the stupendous and cosmogonal philosophy of the Bhagavad Gita in comparison with which our modern world and its literature seem puny and trivial."

If there is one book that has the permanent solution to all the problems that we see in the world and experience in our own lives, it is the Bhagavad Gita. If each person in this world starts following the principles taught in the Bhagavad Gita, most of those issues will never even arise. And, even if we do happen to encounter a problem, we will be so well-prepared that it will have no impact on us. Bold claim? It is. This is, however, a fact.

Following the advice given in this one book alone can keep us happy for the rest of our lives. In fact, we do not even understand what true happiness is; because we have never experienced it. The Bhagavad Gita can guide us in achieving that eternal state of happiness. This one book is enough to cleanse our minds of all negativity and guide us into a paradise of serenity and bliss.

The Bhagavad Gita has all of the answers to all of the questions worth asking that we've had since the beginning of time. Who am I — a body, a mind, a soul? Where have I come from? What exactly is death? What happens after death? Is there a God? Who is God? How does He look like? Why can't I see Him? Is there one God or are there many Gods? Is there a reason for my existence? If so, what is it?

No other book can claim to give answers to humanity's most fundamental questions, such as these.

The Vedas are the world's oldest religious texts. And the Bhagavad Gita is a distillation of the most significant and relevant aspects of the Vedic philosophy. This makes the Bhagavad Gita the oldest philosophy ever. Apart from being the oldest, it is also the most perfect philosophy. It explains how the universe functions, who God is and what is His purpose, and also who we are, and what we are here to do. It also contains the ideal antidote to all the negativity in our lives.

The Bhagavad Gita even depicts how God looks like, and how we can reach Him. Nowhere else do we find a more vivid description of the characteristics of God.

The Bhagavad Gita explains how nature, as a fragment of Krishna, keeps the universe going, what its various forms and traits are, and how we are deceived by the illusions of the material world. It also reveals how the four-fold Yoga system can help us overcome the pains of the material world.

This is the magic of the Bhagavad Gita.

Overall, the Bhagavad Gita is an all-in-one how-to guide for living the most perfect life possible.

To know more about what makes the Bhagavad Gita an ideal philosophy to pursue, you can read my short book (available for free in ebook format) titled *Bhagavad Gita — The Perfect Philosophy*.

Why did the Lord sing the Bhagavad Gita?

This is a common question I get from spiritual seekers:

"Why did Lord Krishna sing the Bhagavad Gita so long after the material world was created? Didn't those who were born before that time need this knowledge?"

This is a good question. And the answer is hidden inside the Bhagavad Gita itself. The Lord reveals in the opening few verses of Chapter 4 of the Bhagavad Gita that the message contained in the Bhagavad Gita was first imparted by Him to the sun-god at the time of the universe's creation and was then passed down in a methodical manner. This shows that sincere seekers have always had access to this knowledge.

The Vedas explain that each time God creates this material world, the age of the world is divided into four periods, called *Yugas*. These are Satya, Treta, Dvapara, and Kali. The Satya-Yuga is characterized by goodness and religion and lasts 1,728,000 years. In the Treta-Yuga, vice is introduced and continues to rise in the Dvapara-Yuga. These yugas last 1,296,000 and 864,000 years, respectively. In the Kali-Yuga (the age we are living in) the ignorance of religion and prevalence of strife reaches its peak and it lasts 432,000 years.

Therefore, the need for such divine knowledge is the greatest in the Kali-Yuga. The Kali-Yuga began as soon as Krishna left this world to go back to His holy abode, Vaikuntha. But, before He left, He wanted to make sure that His real devotees in this dark age of Kali-Yuga had enough support for spiritual progress. So, He contrived this situation so that He could empower future generations with this much-needed divine information.

Bhagavad Gita — A guide beyond religion

Let's be very clear about one thing. The Bhagavad Gita is *not* a religious book. It's a guidebook for life, a how-to manual. The words 'Hindu' or 'Hinduism' appear nowhere in the Bhagavad Gita, or any Vedic scripture for that matter.

Throughout the Bhagavad Gita, Lord Krishna refers to 'beings' rather than 'Hindus.' This is because this song divine is not intended to be read and acted upon by the adherents of a particular religion. This is intended for all people. It is a medicine for the infected souls of the Kali-Yuga. And there is no religion in medicine.

There were no separate religions in the world when the Lord uttered the Bhagavad Gita to Arjuna. Sanatana Dharma, which means 'eternal religion,' was the common religion of all humanity. The primordial religion of mankind is Sanatana Dharma. No matter how many faiths we construct for our own convenience and ego gratification, the reality remains that Sanatana Dharma will always be our actual religion, and Lord Krishna will always be our true object of worship.

As soon as Arjuna realizes this, he says to the Lord, "You are imperishable and the supreme one to be known; You are the ultimate repository of this universe; You are inexhaustible; You are the protector of Sanatana Dharma (the eternal religion); You are the eternal person. This is my opinion." [BG 11.18]

The purpose of this book

Anyone who has studied the Bhagavad Gita knows that it is not the easiest scripture to learn, comprehend, and remember. Even though one has studied this text one verse at a time, it is still necessary to revisit it on a regular basis. Most seekers do not have the time to study religious books daily in today's world. To stay in touch with the divine teachings, one needs a reference guide that may be consulted regularly.

All of this inspired me to create this book, which is intended to accomplish the following goals:

1. Long texts can discourage people from seeking spiritual enlightenment. This book will inspire amateur seekers to dive into this holy pool of wisdom without any qualms.

2. Even when a seeker begins studying this scripture verse by verse, life often gets in the way of his quest for enlightenment. This condensed version will keep the seeker motivated and prevent that from happening.

3. This book will serve as a revision tool for a seeker who has studied the Bhagavad Gita in its entirety but does not have time to revisit it on a regular basis.

4. This book will also serve as a reference for anyone looking for the essence of a particular topic covered by Lord Krishna in the Bhagavad Gita.

5. Many ideas are repeated several times in the Bhagavad Gita. The objective of such repetitions is, of course, to underline vital issues while also communicating the same points in various ways to appeal to diverse types of seekers. However, once a seeker has a complete understanding of a topic, such

repetition becomes unnecessary. This book aims to reduce the number of such repetitions. However, certain essential ideas have still been repeated in places where they were an important aspect of another topic or chapter.

This book is designed as a condensed version of Lord Krishna's sacred dialogue with Arjuna, divided into the same 18 chapters as the original version. I have retained the conversational approach to give the readers a sense of how the discussion evolved, but in a shortened and simpler format. Each chapter concludes with a section titled "Key Takeaways," which highlights all of the key themes presented in the chapter that a seeker should remember.

This book also includes a chapter titled "The Bhagavad Gita in a Nutshell," which includes all the important teachings of the Bhagavad Gita in a point-by-point format grouped by topics. This chapter includes the crux of the entire Bhagavad Gita.

Now, as I believe I have equipped you with everything you might need beforehand, let us now plunge into the summarized and simplified version of this sacred pool of enlightenment known as the Bhagavad Gita.

Chapter 1 - Arjuna's Grief

Dhritarashtra (to Sanjaya): O Sanjaya, please let me know what my own sons, the Kauravas, and the sons of my cousin Pandu, the Pandavas, are doing on the battlefield of Kurukshetra.

Sanjaya (to Dhritarashtra): Seeing the Pandava army drawn up in battle formation, King Duryodhana approached the teacher, Drona, and spoke the following words.

Duryodhana (to Dronacharya): O teacher, look at this massive army of the Pandavas. There are so many great warriors in that army. However, the generals of my army, who are all prepared to lay down their lives for me, are no less skilled in battle. In fact, my army is led by Bhishma and is therefore much better protected than their army being led by Bhima.

Sanjaya (to Dhritarashtra): Then, Grandsire Bhishma blew his conch and thus announced the start of the war, sounding as loud as a lion's roar. Then, from the Kaurava side, a symphony of conchs, kettledrums, tabors, trumpets, and horns erupted, making the environment deafening.

Krishna then blew His heavenly conch. Following that, Arjuna, the other Pandavas, and the warriors on the Pandava side blew their conchs. That uproarious sound reverberated through the sky and the land and shattered the hearts of the Kauravas.

Then Arjuna asked Krishna the following.

Arjuna (to Lord Krishna): O Krishna, please position my chariot between the two armies so that I can survey all of those who are arrayed here desiring to battle in order to please the evil-minded Duryodhana.

Sanjaya (to Dhritarashtra): Hearing that, Krishna drove the grand chariot between the two armies. Within both armies, Arjuna saw many kinsmen, well-wishers, and friends. Thus, overwhelmed with compassion, Arjuna said the following to Krishna.

Arjuna (to Lord Krishna): O Krishna, my limbs are faltering, my mouth has gotten dry, my body is shivering, my hair is standing on end, and my bow is sliding from my hand, as I watch these kinsmen arrayed, ready to fight. I am unable to stand firmly.

Besides, I don't see the point in killing my own kinsmen. What good is dominion, pleasure, or even life to us? Those for whom we yearn for kingship and pleasure stand here in battle. I have no desire to kill them, even though I may be killed by them.

How can we be joyful if we murder our own relatives? I only see devastation and bad omens all around me.

Sanjaya (to Dhritarashtra): After speaking thus, Arjuna, with his mind distressed with grief, casting aside his bow and arrows, sat down on the seat of the chariot.

Key Takeaways

1. Ego never pays off and leads to one's downfall.
2. Being unaware of spiritual realities causes one to become unnecessarily anxious.

Chapter 2 - An Introduction to Yoga

Sanjaya (to Dhritarashtra): Krishna spoke the following words to Arjuna, who was overwhelmed with compassion, having eyes filled with tears.

Lord Krishna (to Arjuna): O Arjuna, in this perilous condition, from where has this impure despondency come upon you, suitable only for unenlightened people? Don't give in to this impotence; it does not suit you. Arise!

Arjuna (to Lord Krishna): O Krishna, how can I direct arrows toward Bhishma and Drona, who are deserving of devotion? It would be better for us to live by begging rather than killing them. By killing these noblemen, our prosperity would be soiled with blood.

I am not sure which would be better — that we shall conquer them or that we should let them conquer us. I am unsure of what I am supposed to do. I implore You to tell me which is the best path for me. Now I am Your disciple and have taken refuge in You. Please guide me.

Sanjaya (to Dhritarashtra): Arjuna then declared to Krishna, "I will not fight," and fell silent. O King, Krishna, as if smiling, then spoke the following words to the grief-stricken Arjuna.

Lord Krishna (to Arjuna): O Arjuna, the wise mourn neither for the dead nor for the living. Never indeed, I did not exist, nor you, nor all these kings; nor will any of us ever cease to exist. As childhood, youth, and old age are for the soul in this body, similar is the attainment of another body. This being so, a man of knowledge is never bewildered by such transitions.

The contacts of senses with the sense-objects produce the temporary notions of heat and cold, pleasure and pain. Thus, bear them without being disturbed. The firm man who is not afflicted by these sensory perceptions is alone deemed eligible for liberation, which is the purpose of human life.

The soul within the body is real and indestructible, whereas the body is an illusion and is impermanent. The soul is eternal and changeless, never taking birth or dying. When the body is slain, the soul is not slain. Therefore, fight!

Just as a person, casting off worn-out clothes, puts on new clothes, in the same way, the soul, discarding decayed bodies, accepts new bodies. The soul is invisible and inconceivable. Therefore, you need not grieve.

All beings are unmanifest before birth, manifest while living in this world, and unmanifest again after death. What is there to grieve about?

Also considering your mandated duty as a *Kshatriya*, a member of the warrior caste, you should not waver; for there is nothing better for a Kshatriya than to fight in a righteous war. You should be happy to have gotten such an opportunity to fight for a righteous cause. However, if you refuse to do your duty, you would be incurring sin. Therefore, fight for the sake of fulfilling your duty.

I would now impart to you the knowledge which will set you free from the bondage of continuous births and deaths in this material world. This knowledge is enlightening. Never doubt it.

Unintelligent men, seeking fulfillment of their material desires, are drawn to the flowery words of the Vedas, considering them to be the only source of wisdom. Such men cannot practice Yoga — the path of getting one with the Supreme.

The Vedas mainly deal with the subject of the modes of material nature. O Arjuna, rise above these modes and the pairs of opposites like pain-pleasure, profit-loss, and so on. Be ever-established in the consciousness of being a soul, free from the ideas of acquisition and preservation of material belongings.

Your right is to perform your duties, but not the rewards of your actions. Never think of yourself as the creator of the rewards of your actions, and never renounce action. Perform your actions without material attachments and the notions of success and failure. This is Karma Yoga — the Yoga of proper action.

Arjuna (to Lord Krishna): O Krishna, what is the description of one who possesses steady wisdom and is thus merged in transcendence?

Lord Krishna (to Arjuna): O Arjuna, one is said to be set in stable wisdom when he entirely gives up all material cravings and is satisfied in himself. A sage of a stable mind is someone who is neither rattled by adversity nor yearns for pleasures and is free of worldly attachments, fear, and anger.

When an even-minded person withdraws his senses from the sense-objects, like a tortoise withdrawing its limbs within the shell, then his intelligence becomes steady.

The objects of sense gratification, while turning away from the one who abstains from them, leave behind the longing for them in his mind. But one who constantly thinks of Me is freed even from the longing. The turbulent senses forcibly carry away one's consciousness, even while he is striving diligently to control those senses. Restraining all his senses, one should concentrate on Me as the Supreme One.

While brooding on sense-objects, a person develops an attachment to them; such attachment produces lust; from lust arises anger because of non-satisfaction; from anger comes delusion due to the resulting mental disturbances; from delusion arises loss of memory about the true identity of oneself; from loss of memory arises loss of the sense of discrimination between the real and the unreal; and from loss of intelligence, one falls down in his spiritual progress.

A person of restraint, on the other hand, can attain peace even while walking amid things of sense pleasure, because his senses are under control, and he is free of both attraction and repulsion. A steady mind is a must for peace and happiness.

That person attains peace into whom all desires enter, just like the waters enter the ocean, which remains ever undisturbed even while continually being filled; not the one who savors such desires.

O Arjuna, this is the state of being established in the Supreme Being. Being established in this state, one never gets deluded. Becoming thus situated, even at the moment of death, one attains oneness with Me, the Supreme One.

Key Takeaways

1. All beings are actually eternal souls. We are born, live, die, and then are born again. This cycle continues until we attain liberation from it, which is the purpose of human life.
2. When our senses come into contact with material nature, our minds are filled with a variety of sensory perceptions. Such fleeting sense experiences never bother an enlightened person.
3. It is never advisable to avoid performing one's obligatory duties, as this results in sin.
4. The outcome is never in one's control, so one should never be concerned about it. Instead, one should concentrate on doing his work efficiently.
5. It is essential to stay free of material desires and unattached to sense-objects at all times. One of the most significant roadblocks to spiritual growth is a desire for sensual pleasures. Rather, one should concentrate on Krishna and cultivate a desire to reach Him.

Chapter 3 - The Yoga of Action

Arjuna (to Lord Krishna): O Krishna, if knowledge is considered by You to be superior to activities, why then do You want to engage me in this heinous activity? You are confusing me with these contradictory statements. Please tell me decisively that *one* best way for me.

Lord Krishna (to Arjuna): Jnana Yoga or Sankhya Yoga — Yoga of knowledge — is for the wise, and Karma Yoga — Yoga of action — is for the Karma Yogis.

One cannot attain freedom from action by merely abstaining from work. No one can ever remain, even for a moment, without performing action, because everyone is compelled to act by the traits they have inherited from material nature.

One who restrains the organs of action but keeps thinking of sense-objects is a hypocrite. But, one who disciplines the senses, O Arjuna, and engages oneself in Karma Yoga without regard for the outcome excels.

Perform your prescribed duties, because action is superior to inaction. Even the maintenance of your body is not possible through inaction. But keep in mind that actions, other than those performed as an offering to Me, result in bondage. Therefore, devote your actions to Me.

At the beginning of creation, Brahma said to humanity, "By sacrifice shall you prosper." Nourish the gods with sacrifice; the gods, in return, will nourish you with the reward of the sacrifice. Thus, by nourishing one another, you will attain Me. But, he who enjoys what has been given by the gods without offering in return to them, is indeed a thief.

Sages who consume the food that is first offered as a sacrifice to the gods are cleansed of all sins; whereas selfish people who prepare food for their own pleasure incur sin.

Keep performing your prescribed duties without attachment to their outcomes. By doing so, one attains Me.

You should also carry out your responsibilities in order to prevent the common people from ruining their own lives by remaining uninformed about proper behavior. Every action taken by a superior is replicated by the common man.

Even though I have no work assigned to me and nothing to gain, I take action. Because if I ever fail to participate in continuous action, all men will mimic My manner, destroying the entire universe.

A wise man, however, should never upset the minds of those who are fixated on the potential rewards of their activities. Rather, by working with devotion himself, he should motivate them to perform their tasks without regard for material gain.

While all actions are actually carried out by the attributes of material nature, one whose intelligence is deluded by ego thinks "I am the doer." But, he who knows the truth about the different modes of material nature and how they work, and knows that these attributes exist in both the senses and the sense-objects, never becomes attached.

Those who constantly follow these instructions of Mine faithfully, without unnecessary fault-finding, become free from the bondage of material actions. Those who ignore these lessons, on the other hand, are doomed in their spiritual pursuits.

Attachment and aversion toward sense-objects generate from the senses. One should not come under the influence of the senses.

It is preferable to execute one's own responsibility even if it is of poor quality, than to perform another's duty well.

Arjuna (to Lord Krishna): Then, O Krishna, by what is one driven to commit sinful activities, even against his will, as though forced?

Lord Krishna (to Arjuna): It is the desire that one should know to be an enemy. As fire is obscured by smoke, as a mirror by dust, and as the embryo by the womb, so is one's intelligence covered by desire. Think of material desire as fire that is never satisfied, even after destroying everything.

Desire dwells in the senses, the mind, and the intellect. Through all these, it deludes the soul by eclipsing its wisdom. Therefore, control the senses and slay this sinful destroyer of wisdom called desire.

Key Takeaways

1. One should never be attached to inaction, but should always strive to perform his duties well.
2. Nature compels everyone to act, therefore evading one's responsibilities is not a wise idea.
3. One should dedicate all actions and their outcomes to Krishna.
4. Material nature is the real doer. One should never, out of ego, consider oneself to be the principal controller of one's activities and their outcomes.

5. One should always be aware of the material desires arising in one's mind and should be careful not to indulge in their fulfillment, as that ultimately leads to spiritual failure.

Chapter 4 - The Yoga of Knowledge

Lord Krishna (to Arjuna): I taught this imperishable Yoga — the science of getting one with Me — to Vivasvan, the sun-god; Vivasvan taught it to Manu, the father of humankind, and Manu passed it on to Ikshvaku, the founder of the solar dynasty in which I appeared as Rama. This supreme knowledge was thus handed down through orderly succession. But, by the long lapse of time, the great Yoga was lost, O Arjuna. I am teaching that same ancient Yoga to you, as you are My devotee as well as My friend. This knowledge is a supreme secret.

Arjuna (to Lord Krishna): Your birth was later; Vivasvan was born earlier. How am I to understand that You instructed thus to Vivasvan at the beginning of creation?

Lord Krishna (to Arjuna): O Arjuna! Many births of Mine have passed, and also yours. I know them all, but you not.

Although I am unborn and eternal and am the Lord of all beings, yet subjugating My own divine nature, I incarnate in My own way. Whenever there is a decline in virtue and a rise in vice, I manifest Myself. For protecting the pious and annihilating the wicked, and thus to reestablish righteousness, I appear in every era. One who truly understands the divine nature of My appearance and activities does not take birth again in this material world; he comes to Me.

Most humans, unaware of My nature, worship the demigods by offering sacrifices, desiring the fruits of their efforts, because in this mortal world, so-called success is obtained quickly through result-oriented work.

According to the modes of nature and the related activities, I constructed the four-fold caste system, which includes the Brahmins (religious leaders), Kshatriyas (rulers and defenders), Vaishyas (merchants and farmers), and Shudras (laborers). But, even though I created that system, know Me as a non-doer and immutable since I am not a part of it.

I am not tainted by action, and I have no desire for the rewards of actions. One who knows Me thus does not become entangled by actions.

A wise man performs only bodily activities with no expectation of reward, with his mind and intellect under control, and having given up any sense of ownership of material belongings, and thus commits no sin. Being free of envy and content with what comes to him of its own accord, having transcended the conceptions of dualities such as success-failure, gain-loss, rich-poor, and so on, a wise man performs actions, but is not bound by their reactions. All the deeds of a man who is unattached to the outcomes of his actions, whose mind is rooted in wisdom, and who acts as a sacrifice offered to Me disintegrate completely, leaving no trace in his subsequent incarnations.

Some Yogis (those who pursue oneness with the Supreme God) vow to use their senses purely for spiritual pursuits, while others vow to avoid all sense-objects. Others propose wealth, penances, and knowledge development as sacrifices. Yet others restrict their diet as a kind of sacrifice. All these Yogis destroy their sins through sacrifices. Even this material world is not for the non-performer of sacrifices; what to say of the divine world?

Remember that the sacrifice of knowledge (the practice of acquiring divine wisdom) is superior to the sacrifice of material objects alone.

Know that through surrender, inquiry, and service, the wise seers of truth will impart that knowledge to you, knowing which, you will never again come under such delusion, and by which you will see all beings being of the same nature as yourself, and also as a part of Me. Therefore, seek knowledge from a wise sage.

Even if you are the worst of all sinners, the boat of knowledge will undoubtedly enable you to traverse the ocean of sins. Similar to how a blazing fire turns firewood to ashes, the fire of knowledge reduces all material reactions to ashes. Knowledge is the best cleanser in the world. In time, a person who has mastered Yoga will discover such knowledge inside himself.

A man full of faith, who is dedicated to the attainment of transcendental knowledge, attains it. Thereafter, he quickly attains the supreme peace of self-realization. On the other hand, one who is ignorant and faithless, and has a doubting mind, perishes in his spiritual endeavors. For a person of doubting mind, there is neither this material world, nor the spiritual world, nor the supreme bliss.

Key Takeaways

1. The knowledge imparted by Lord Krishna in the Bhagavad Gita is the oldest knowledge intended for humankind, having been given by Him at the inception of the universe. This establishes Krishna as the Supreme God and the Bhagavad Gita as the repository of supreme knowledge.

2. Lord Krishna is the Supreme eternal being. Still, he incarnates in various forms and times to restore righteousness in this world.

3. A man of knowledge performs actions just for survival, not to accumulate wealth and possessions.

4. The qualities of one's actions (karma) determine the quality of his next birth. A man of knowledge is not bound by such reactions of karma and attains Krishna after leaving the body.

5. Various kinds of sacrifices are prescribed that cleanse one's karma and purify one's mind, making one fit for liberation.

6. A Yogi should ideally approach a wise sage and obtain divine knowledge under his guidance.

7. Doubts are hindrances to spiritual advancement, and one should get rid of them as quickly as possible.

Chapter 5 - True Renunciation

Arjuna (to Lord Krishna): O Krishna, You praise both renunciation of activities as well as the Yoga of action — Karma Yoga. Please tell me which of these two is the better route.

Lord Krishna (to Arjuna): Karma Yoga and renunciation of action both lead to liberation. But, of the two, Karma Yoga is superior. One who neither hates nor craves the rewards of his activities and objects of sense enjoyment should be regarded as being constantly renounced because he is free from the bondage of material work.

The ignorant, not the wise, regard Jnana Yoga as being different from Karma Yoga. One who is fully established in even one of these receives the rewards of both. One who sees these two at the same level sees the truth.

But, O Arjuna, renunciation is difficult to achieve without Karma Yoga. He who acts without attachment to results, dedicating his actions to Me, is not tainted by sin, just as the lotus leaf is unaffected by water. The Karma Yogis use their bodies, minds, intellects, and senses only to purify themselves by directing their activities toward self-realization. This is how they achieve true peace.

I neither create the illusion of being a doer of activities for the people of the world, nor do I cause them to do activities, nor do I entangle them in the outcomes of their actions. It is material nature that causes all these.

I do not accept anyone's sin, or even virtue, because it is the role of Karma, not Me, to account for one's vice and virtue. Ignorance eclipses knowledge, leading to deception. But, knowledge, like the sun, reveals the Supreme Truth to those whose ignorance is dissolved by self-awareness.

Those whose soul is one with Me, whose faith is given to Me, who have made Me their greatest goal, and whose sins have been cleansed through pure knowledge, reach the state of liberation from material births and deaths.

The intelligent, gifted with wisdom and humility, view a Brahmin, a cow, an elephant, a dog, and even an outcast with equal regard. This is the mark of a wise sage who has attained enlightenment. Such an even-minded man does not celebrate when he obtains something pleasant, nor does he lament when he obtains something unpleasant.

One whose mind is not attached to external objects of pleasure finds joy within oneself. Meditating on Me, he enjoys eternal bliss. The pleasure derived from sensory interactions with nature ultimately leads to misery, since it is transient. Such pleasure does not excite the wise. A Yogi is someone who can resist the urges of want and wrath and is thus always happy.

Shutting out all contacts with sense-objects, fixing his vision between the two eyebrows, and making even the inward and outward breaths moving within the nostrils, controlling the senses, mind, and intelligence, the sage solely aiming at liberation, free from desire, fear, and anger, certainly attains eternal liberation.

One who knows Me as the ultimate beneficiary of all sacrifices and austerities, the Supreme Lord of all worlds, and the friend of all beings, attains eternal peace through liberation.

Key Takeaways

1. Giving up one's responsibilities is not the same as renunciation. True renunciation is disinterest toward objects of pleasure, the rewards for one's actions, and negative emotions such as greed and anger.
2. Actions performed with such sense of renunciation and dedicated to Krishna do not

bind one to this material world and provide true peace.

3. Knowledge is also crucial for a Yogi. A wise and even-minded person, knowing that all beings are pure spirit souls, views all beings with an equal eye.

4. Free from dualities, a true Yogi is neither excited by positive outcomes nor disappointed by negative outcomes. He always remains the same.

5. A man of knowledge constantly meditates on Krishna, which opens for him the doors to divine bliss.

6. A true Yogi knows Krishna to be the Supreme Person and the Lord of the universe.

Chapter 6 - The Yoga of Meditation

Lord Krishna (to Arjuna): A renunciate and a Yogi is one who executes his responsibilities without regard for the benefits, not one who is ignorant and inactive.

In all situations, stay grounded in self-awareness and connected to Me. The mind is the best friend of a person whose knowledge of the self has conquered the mind. An unconquered mind remains an enemy of the soul.

A Yogi should live in a peaceful environment and maintain a constant focus on Me with a controlled mind and body. His seat should be sturdy, neither too high nor too low, and covered first with grass, then with deer or tiger skin, and finally with a cloth, and he should sit in a clean spot. He should practice Dhyana Yoga — Yoga of meditation — sitting there with a single-pointed mind, controlling the activities of the mind and the senses, for the cleansing of the soul, making it fit for liberation.

The Yogi should sit, meditating on Me as the Supreme Goal, holding his body, neck, and head erect and still, being stable, gazing at the tip of his nose without glancing around, being tranquil in mind, and resolute in the vow of celibacy. As a result, the self-balanced Yogi achieves peace, which leads to liberation.

Dhyana Yoga is not for those who eat or sleep too much or too little, O Arjuna. For one who is moderate in his habits of eating, recreation, and sleep, and moderate in efforts in work, Dhyana Yoga becomes the destroyer of pain.

A lamp does not flicker if it is placed in a windless spot. This metaphor could be applied to describe a Yogi who has learned to control his thoughts through meditation.

When a Yogi restrains and quietens his mind through the practice of Dhyana Yoga, and thus sees himself as a soul, finding contentment in that fact, thus experiencing immeasurable bliss of contact with Me through transcendental awareness, he becomes established in truth.

That state of self-realization, once obtained, is considered by the Yogi as the gain beyond all other gains; established in which he remains unshaken even in the mightiest misery. That stage is known as Yoga — the stage of freedom from pain.

This Yoga should be practiced with determination and a resolute mind. Whenever the restless mind wanders, the Yogi must withdraw it from all distractions and bring it back under the control of the knowledge of the soul.

With the mind absorbed in the Yoga of meditation, the Yogi sees Me in all beings and all beings in Me. Indeed, he sees My existence everywhere. One who sees Me everywhere, and sees everything in Me, never loses Me, nor is he ever lost to Me. He who, realizing the sameness of the souls, O Arjuna, sees equality all around, in both joy and sorrow, is the best kind of Yogi.

Arjuna (to Lord Krishna): Due to restlessness of the mind, O Krishna, I do not see how this Yoga of equanimity through meditation on the soul and the Supreme Soul, that has been explained by You, can have an enduring effect. The mind is restless, turbulent, powerful, and stubborn. I consider it as difficult to control as the wind.

Lord Krishna (to Arjuna): Undoubtedly, O Arjuna, the mind is restless and difficult to regulate; yet, it can be controlled through the practice of the Yoga of meditation and dispassion.

Arjuna (to Lord Krishna): O Krishna, what happens to one who is unsuccessful in Yoga — who in the beginning had taken to Yoga with faith, but later was unable to control himself, as his mind wandered away from Yoga?

Lord Krishna (to Arjuna): No one who does good ever meets misfortune. The fallen Yogi, after entering the heavenly worlds, and living there for several years, is again born in this world in the home of the righteous and the rich, or in the family of wise Yogis. Such a birth is hard to obtain.

There, he recovers the wisdom acquired in former lives and strives harder than before for spiritual perfection. By virtue of his practice of Yoga in his previous lives, he is carried forward in his path toward perfection. And, by striving diligently, the reborn fallen Yogi, purified of all karmic sins, finally attaining perfection after the efforts of many lives, attains the supreme goal of My association.

A Yogi who constantly meditates on Me is superior to the so-called ascetic who does not pursue Me. He is also superior to the men of theoretical knowledge and to the men of mere action with a desire for rewards. Therefore, strive to be a Yogi by the practice of meditating on Me, O Arjuna.

Of all types of Yogis, the one who, being full of faith, merging his soul in Me, worships Me — I regard him as the most devout Yogi.

Key Takeaways

1. One must always remain conscious of the fact of being a soul and being a part of the Supreme Soul, Krishna.

2. A Yogi should sit firm in a quiet spot, with a focused mind, and practice Dhyana Yoga — the Yoga of meditation.

3. A Yogi must be moderate in his habits of eating, sleeping, and recreation. He should also be careful not to overstress his body or mind, as this will make it unsuited for Yoga.

4. A Yogi sees the presence of the same Supreme Soul in all beings.

5. A Yogi who fails in his practice goes to heavenly planets after death, and thereafter is reborn in this world in conditions conducive to spiritual advancement. Thus, progressing through several lives, he ultimately reaches Krishna's abode to stay there forever.

Chapter 7 - The Supreme and His Nature

Lord Krishna (to Arjuna): Among thousands of men, perhaps one strives for perfection by knowing Me; and among those few who diligently strive for perfection, perhaps one is able to comprehend My nature, powers, and personality.

Earth, water, fire, air, space, mind, intelligence, and ego — these eight elements make up My material nature which flows into the material world. This is My inferior nature. Different from it is My superior nature — the soul.

Know that these two natures of Mine comprise the source of everything. Understand that I am the creator as well as the annihilator of the entire universe. There is nothing superior to Me, O Arjuna. All beings and objects are strung in Me, as a row of gems on a thread.

I am the taste of water; I am the light of the moon and the sun; I am the syllable 'om' in all the divine Vedic hymns; the sound in space; and virility in men. I am the sweet fragrance of the earth; and I am the radiance in the fire; the life in all beings; and the penance in the ascetics. I am the intelligence of the intelligent, the splendor of the splendid, and the strength of the strong.

Know that all beings and objects, be they of pure, passionate, or dark modes of nature, emanate from Me. The entire world, deluded by these three modes (purity, passion, and darkness) of material nature, does not understand Me to be beyond and above these modes, and as inexhaustible. Indeed, this divine illusion of Mine, consisting of the three modes of material nature, is difficult to cross over. Only those who take refuge in Me can cross over this illusion. The miscreants and the deluded ones, whose wisdom is stolen by material illusion, who follow the path of demonic beings by living immorally, do not seek refuge in Me.

Four kinds of virtuous men worship Me — the distressed, the seekers of knowledge, the seekers of wealth, and the wise ones who know My real nature. Of them, the wise, ever engaged in My devotion, is the best; for I am very dear to the wise, and he is dear to Me. After many births and deaths, the wise man attains Me, realizing Me to be everything. Such a great soul is very rare.

Those whose intelligence has been hijacked by the various kinds of material desires worship the other gods (demigods), following the particular demigod's injunctions, according to their own natures. I make a devotee's faith in whatever demigod he wishes to worship unwavering, rather than compelling him to worship Me directly. Endowed with that faith, the deluded worshipper engages in the worship of that demigod, and from that worship gains fulfillment of his desires. However, in reality, these satisfactions of desires are arranged by Me alone.

Remember that the rewards gained by the worshipers of the demigods are perishable. The worshipers of the demigods go to the abodes of the respective demigods after death before again being reborn in the material world. On the other hand, My devotees come to Me and stay with Me eternally.

The unintelligent ones think of Me as the unmanifest who has manifested by taking a human-like body, oblivious to My greater nature, which is imperishable and sublime, and thus think of Me as an ordinary god or incarnation. I am not manifest to all, veiled by My assumed human-like nature. The deluded world does not know Me as the unborn and the imperishable Supreme God.

O Arjuna, I know all the beings of the past, the present, and the future; but Me no one knows.

At birth, all beings are immersed into delusion, forgetting the spiritual truths about themselves and Me, bewildered by the dualities arising from the feelings of likes and dislikes. In this way, the dualities bind beings to material nature.

But men of good actions, whose sins have been entirely cleansed and who have been freed from the deception of duality, worship Me with unwavering devotion.

Those who strive for liberation from old age and death, taking refuge in Me, know Me as Brahman — the Supreme God. They know everything about the soul — *Adhyatma*, and also about actions — *Karma*. Those who perceive Me in the physical manifestations — as *Adhibhuta*, in the godly beings — as *Adhidaiva*, and also as the beneficiary of sacrifices — as *Adhiyajna*, can perceive Me even at the time of death.

Key Takeaways

1. Rare is the person who is able to see past the illusory nature of this material world, perceives Krishna as the Supreme Being, and pursues Him as his supreme goal.
2. The material world is formed of Krishna's inferior material nature. However, His superior nature is also present here in all beings as souls.

3. Krishna is the creator, maintainer, and destroyer of the entire universe, and is present in everything and everyone.

4. The deluded beings worship the demigods, oblivious to the fact that Krishna is the Supreme God. The benefits people obtain from worshiping the other gods are temporary. Those who worship Krishna, on the other hand, attain Him and are blessed with His everlasting companionship.

5. All beings forget their actual nature and Krishna when they are born, and they become trapped in their various likes and dislikes. Such dualities bind beings to the material world. But those whose effects of karma have been negated by rewards or punishments through multiple lifetimes, become enlightened again about their spiritual truths, and attain liberation through loving devotion to Krishna.

Chapter 8 - The Imperishable Supreme

Arjuna (to Lord Krishna): O Supreme Person! What is *Brahman*? What is *Adhyatma*? What is *Karma*? What is *Adhibhuta*? What is *Adhidaiva*? What is *Adhiyajna*, and how *Adhiyajna* dwells in the material body? And how, at the time of death, can a self-disciplined devotee know You?

Lord Krishna (to Arjuna): I am *Brahman* — the indestructible and Supreme God. My essential nature is *Adhyatma* — the individual soul. Action causing material beings to take birth by binding them to the material world is known as *Karma*. *Adhibhuta* is the perishable physical body. *Adhidaiva* is the divine consciousness of the Supreme Person dwelling in the demigods. And I, the Spirit within the body of everyone and everything in the universe, being the object of all sacrifices and devotion, am also known as *Adhiyajna*.

Whatever state of being is prevalent in one's mind at the time of death, O Arjuna, that very state he will acquire in his next life, because of his persistent thought of it. Therefore, remember Me at all times. You will undoubtedly achieve Me if you devote your mind and intelligence solely to Me.

He who, with a single-pointed mind, is engaged in Abhyasa Yoga — the Yoga of practice of meditation on Me — reaches Me. One who meditates upon Me — the Omniscient, the Ancient, the Controller, smaller than the atom, the maintainer of all, of inconceivable form, luminous like the sun, beyond the darkness of ignorance — at the time of death, engaged fully in devotion, by regular practice of meditation, certainly attains Me. There is no doubt about this.

After attaining Me, the highest perfection, the great souls never take birth again in this temporary place full of miseries. O Arjuna, all material worlds up to the world of Brahma, the most senior of all created gods, are subject to repeated births and deaths. But upon reaching Me, one does not take birth again in the material world.

Those who know the duration of a day of Brahma, My Creator Form, which lasts a thousand ages, and the duration of a night of Brahma, which also lasts a thousand ages, they truly know 'day' and 'night.' At the coming of Brahma's day, all beings become manifest from the unmanifest state; and at the coming of Brahma's night, they dissolve into the unmanifest state again.

But there exists another Unmanifested nature — My divine abode, transcendental to material nature. My abode is eternal and is not annihilated when the mortal world is annihilated. Reaching My abode is the highest goal, attaining which one never returns to this mundane material world.

I, within whom all beings dwell, and by whom the entire existence is pervaded, can be attained by unalloyed devotion alone.

Key Takeaways

1. Krishna is the Supreme God who lives as a soul in all living beings. He is also found in all demigods and is the ultimate beneficiary of all sacrifices.
2. Karma is material action, and the effects of that action bind living beings to this material world.
3. The next life of a living being is decided by the prevalent state of his mind at the time of death. One can only reach Krishna if He remains prevalent in one's mind at the time of death.
4. By regular practice of meditation on Krishna and rendering devotional services to Him, one can establish Him in his mind.
5. All worlds, including the worlds of gods, are subject to creation and annihilation. The material worlds manifest at the arrival of Brahma's day and annihilate at the arrival of Brahma's night. Brahma's one day and one

night last for a thousand ages each. But Krishna's divine abode is transcendental to this cycle and is eternal.

6. One who reaches Krishna's abode never returns to the material world. This is the goal of human life.

Chapter 9 - The Royal Secret

Lord Krishna (to Arjuna): Since you do not focus on finding faults unnecessarily, I will now reveal to you this most secret knowledge that will free you from the sufferings of this material existence. This timeless wisdom is the king of education, the highest secret, the supreme purifier, and its practice brings endless bliss.

Those who do not believe in their eternal responsibility to strive for self-realization and liberation, O Arjuna, do not reach Me and keep returning to the material world, where they continue to be born and die.

I pervade the entire cosmos in My unmanifested form. All beings exist in Me, but My all-powerful Self is not situated in them. Only a tiny fraction of Me exists in material beings.

At the end of the cosmic cycle, all beings merge into My nature. I create them again at the start of the next cycle. This is a never-ending loop. All beings and objects are created under My direction by this material nature. This is how the material nature revolves in cycles of Brahma's days and nights.

When I assume the human form, the ignorant fools ridicule Me, unaware of My supreme nature as the Great Lord of all beings.

But the realized souls, taking shelter of My divine nature, devote themselves to Me, knowing that I am the eternal source of all existence. They are always engaged in worshipping Me with devotion, reciting My glories, striving with determination to serve Me, bowing before Me in adoration.

I am the rite, the sacrifice, the oblation to the ancestors, the healing herb, and the sacred chant. I am also the clarified butter used in the sacrificial fire, the sacrificial fire itself, and the oblation put into the fire. I am the father of this entire universe, the mother, the support, and the oldest ancestor. I am the all-inclusive object of knowledge, the purifier, the cosmic syllable *om*, as well as the Rig, the Sama, and the Yajur Vedas. I am the goal, the maintainer, the Lord, the witness, the abode, the refuge, the dearest friend, the origin, the annihilation, the foundation, the divine treasure-house, and the imperishable seed. I am the controller of heat and rain. I am immortality, and also death. I am both the spirit and the physical body.

The virtuous ones, following the instructions given in the Vedas, enter godly worlds after death. After enjoying there, till the merits of their good karma are exhausted, they return to the mortal world. Thus, they, seeking sense pleasures to be enjoyed in the heavenly worlds, as rewards of righteous acts in the material world, achieve only coming and going between the heavens and the earth.

On the other hand, I strengthen the devotion of those who meditate on and worship Me alone, allowing them to attain Me.

Even the devotees of other gods worship Me only, O Arjuna, but in the wrong way. As a result, they are forced to return to this planet.

The devotees of the demigods go to the demigods after death; the devotees of the ancestors go to the ancestors; the devotees of the ghosts go to the ghosts; but My devotees come to Me to stay with Me forever, unlike others who return to this mortal world.

I accept any offering made with devotion by a pure soul, even if it is a simple leaf, a flower, a fruit, water, or anything else.

Whatever you do, whatever you eat, whatever you offer in sacrifice, whatever you give in charity, whatever austerities you undertake — do that as an offering to Me. Thus, you will be liberated from the bondage of actions that forces one to be born in this world again and again.

Those who worship Me with devotion live in Me, and I live in them. Thus, they merge with Me.

Even if a man of abominable conduct worships Me alone, he should be regarded as a sage, because he is rightly resolved. Such a devotee soon becomes righteous and attains eternal peace.

O Arjuna, declare to all with confidence that My devotee never perishes.

Key Takeaways

1. Cynics who are more interested in spotting flaws than improving their knowledge can never attain true wisdom.
2. Krishna is everything and pervades the entire universe. Everything and everyone exist in Krishna. And a tiny fraction of Krishna exists in every person in the form of a soul.
3. One should never think of Krishna as an ordinary god. He is the Supreme One and is above all.
4. One who is always engaged in the devotion of Krishna can attain Him easily.
5. The devotees of the other gods also worship Krishna indirectly. But this is not the recommended way of worshipping Him.

6. One need not offer riches to Krishna. Krishna accepts the simplest of offerings made by His devotees with a pure heart and loving devotion.
7. Devotion to Krishna purifies a person of all sins and leads him to godhood.

Chapter 10 - The Glories of the Divine One

Lord Krishna (to Arjuna): Neither the demigods nor the great sages know My origin. I am the origin of the demigods and the great sages. He who knows Me as the unborn and the beginningless, and also as the Supreme Lord of all the worlds, is wise among humans and free of all sins.

Intelligence, knowledge, non-delusion, forgiveness, truthfulness, control of the senses, control of the mind, happiness, sorrow, birth, death, fear, fearlessness, non-injury to the innocent, equanimity, contentment, austerity, charity, fame, infamy — all these attributes of beings arise from Me alone.

The seven great sages to whom the Vedas were first revealed, the four sons of Brahma, and the fourteen Manus (progenitors of mankind) were all born of My mind, and all beings of the world originate from them. One who knows this opulent nature and mystical personality of Mine becomes unshakably united to Me by becoming liberated.

With minds fixed in meditating on Me, with lives devoted to worshipping Me, enlightening one another by always conversing about Me, My devotees derive contentment and bliss.

Arjuna (to Lord Krishna): You are the Supreme Brahman, the supreme abode, the supreme purifier. You are the eternal person, the divine, the original Lord — the unborn, the omnipresent. All the great sages confirm this, and now You Yourself are declaring this to me.

I totally accept as truth all that You have told me, O Krishna. Indeed, neither the gods nor the demons, O Lord, can understand Your divine personality.

Kindly tell me in detail of Your divine glories — the very glories by which You exist pervading all these worlds. How shall I know You, O Supreme Mystic? In what all forms should I think of You? Please tell me in detail about Your mystic power and opulence. I can never be fully satisfied hearing Your nectar-like words.

Lord Krishna (to Arjuna): O Arjuna! I will certainly tell you My divine glories, but only the most prominent ones, because My opulence has no end.

I am the Supreme Soul, which dwells in the hearts of all beings, and I am the beginning, middle, and end of all living beings. I am the greatest of gods, the greatest of Vedas, the greatest of senses, the greatest of sages, the greatest of words, the greatest of hymns, the highest nature, the greatest of beings, the most powerful of weapons, the most divine, the purest, the highest knowledge, the most sublime, the most valiant warrior.

There is no limit to My divine glories. All this is a mere indication of the expanse of those glories.

But, O Arjuna, what is the need for you to know all this in such detail? It is sufficient to simply understand that I support this entire universe with merely a single fragment of Myself.

Key Takeaways

1. Being outside the dimensions of time, Lord Krishna is unborn and eternal. And whoever understands this is wise.
2. Lord Krishna is the source of all human emotions and traits.
3. Lord's devotees take pleasure in worshipping Him, chanting His holy names, and discussing His greatness and pastimes. Such devotees are the most fortunate ones among humans. They are always eager to learn more about Krishna.
4. Lord's glories are immeasurable and are not possible for us, as humans, to comprehend. We

can only understand a tiny fraction of His divine nature.

5. Lord Krishna must be known as the Supreme One, superior to all other beings and gods.

Chapter 11 - The Universal Form of God

Arjuna (to Lord Krishna): By hearing the highest secret about the Supreme Self uttered by You, my delusion has been dispelled.

O Supreme Lord! I wish to see Your all-encompassing divine form. If You believe I am capable of seeing it, please show me Your universal form.

Lord Krishna (to Arjuna): Behold, O Arjuna, hundreds and thousands of My divine forms having various colors and shapes. Behold all the demigods in Me and also the many wonders never seen before. Behold the entire universe together in My body, including all beings and objects, and whatever else you wish to see.

But you cannot see Me with your limited vision. I am giving you divine eyes. Behold My mystical opulence with those.

Sanjaya (to Dhritarashtra): O King, having spoken thus, the Supreme Lord displayed His supreme opulent form to Arjuna — having many mouths and eyes, adorned with many divine ornaments, holding many divine uplifted weapons, wearing divine garlands and dresses, anointed with divine fragrances — wonderful, brilliant, unlimited, and looking in all directions.

If a thousand suns were present in the sky at the same time, that combined radiance might resemble the effulgence of that Supreme Self. In that gigantic body of the God of gods, Arjuna saw the entire universe in one place.

Then, Arjuna, overwhelmed with wonder, with hairs standing on end, bowed to the Lord, and with joined palms, spoke thus to Krishna.

Arjuna (to Lord Krishna): O Lord, I see all the gods and all classes of beings in Your body. I also see Lord Brahma and all the sages. I see Your endless form on all sides, having countless arms, bellies, mouths, and eyes, and having no beginning, middle, or end. I see You with crowns, clubs, and discs; a mass of effulgence glowing all around, very difficult to see.

You are indestructible and the supreme one. You are limitless. You are the protector of *Sanatana Dharma* — the common eternal religion of mankind. You are the eternal person. You are infinite in power. I see You having the moon and the sun as eyes, with blazing fire coming out from Your mouth, heating the entire universe by Your own radiance. You pervade the entire universe.

The different classes of gods and demons are beholding You in wonder. O Supreme Soul, after seeing Your incomprehensible, wonderful, and terrible form, all the worlds are perturbed and terrified.

All those highly revered gods are entering into You. Some of them, out of fear, extol You with joined palms. Hosts of great sages and perfected beings are praising You with sublime hymns, saying, "May it be well!"

I am terrified seeing Your huge cosmic form touching the sky, blazing with many colors, open-mouthed, with large fiery eyes. Seeing Your many mouths with terrible teeth, looking like the fire of death which dissolves everything into itself, I have lost my sense of direction, and cannot find comfort and steadiness.

Also, all these sons of Dhritarashtra, along with the many kings, Bhishma, Drona, and Karna, with our own prominent warriors, are rapidly entering into Your mouths that have terrible teeth. Some of them are seen sticking in the gaps between the teeth, with their heads crushed. All creatures of the world are dashing into Your mouths as moths rush hastily into a blazing fire for their own destruction.

Obeisances unto You, O Supreme God. Please be gracious and tell me who You are.

Lord Krishna (to Arjuna): I am time, the all-powerful destroyer of the worlds. Even without you, all the warriors arrayed in these confronting armies will perish. Therefore, get up and fight. All of them have already been killed by Me. You ought to be merely an instrument, O Arjuna.

Sanjaya (to Dhritarashtra): After hearing these words of Krishna, the trembling Arjuna, with joined palms, prostrating himself, bowing down, overwhelmed with fear, said again to Krishna with a faltering voice.

Arjuna (to Lord Krishna): It is proper, O Krishna, that the world rejoices in and is drawn to Your glories; that the demons, out of Your fear, run in all directions; and that all groups of the perfected sages bow down in Your honor.

And why should not they pay homage to You, the supreme creator, who is even greater than Brahma? O limitless one, O God of gods, O shelter of the universe! You are the eternal one, the manifest, the unmanifest, and the transcendental. You are the primal God, the oldest person. You are the knower of everything and the only one worthy of being known. You are the Lord of all beings.

Salutation! Salutation be unto You a thousand times, again and again! Salutation to You from all sides indeed, O Everything; You are infinite in power and prowess; You pervade everything. You are everything. When there is no one equal to You, how can there be anyone superior to You?

Whatever I said rashly to You, not knowing Your greatness, regarding You as only a friend, either out of carelessness, or out of love, addressing You as, "O Krishna," "O Yadava," "O friend," and, howsoever I may have insulted You, for all that I beg pardon of You.

I am delighted after seeing Your universal form that has never before been seen. But my mind is unsettled with fear of seeing such a horrible form of Yours. Therefore, O Lord, please show me Your previous form. I wish to behold You as before. Please appear thus.

Lord Krishna (to Arjuna): Becoming free from fear, pleased in mind again, behold this earlier form of Mine.

Sanjaya (to Dhritarashtra): Thus, Krishna again displayed His previous form and reassured the terrified Arjuna by becoming serene again.

Arjuna (to Lord Krishna): O Krishna, seeing this serene, human-like form of Yours, I am now composed in mind and restored to my non-fearful nature.

Lord Krishna (to Arjuna): My universal form is very difficult to behold. Even the gods are always longing to see it.

I cannot be seen in this form by studying the Vedas, nor by undergoing penances, nor by doing charity, nor even by making sacrifices. But only through unwavering devotion, O Arjuna, can I be known and seen in this form.

Key Takeaways

1. The universal form of Krishna encompasses everything that exists.
2. Human eyes are incapable of seeing Krishna in His universal form. Even gods and demons do not have the privilege of seeing that form.
3. Krishna's universal form is all-wonderful, all-brilliant, and unlimited.
4. Even the gods who are otherwise highly regarded by humans can be seen inside Krishna's colossal form.
5. Cynics and doubters, not realizing His supreme nature, always regard Krishna as an ordinary person or god.
6. Krishna's universal form, though divine, is terribly dreadful to view for us as humans. Among all else, the beholder can see in that form awful deaths unfolding that can easily terrify a human mind. That is why it is much easier for us to worship the Lord in His all-

attractive, beautiful, and serene form as Krishna.

7. In the present age, devotion to Krishna is a must in order to know and reach Him.

Chapter 12 - The Yoga of Devotion

Arjuna (to Lord Krishna): O Krishna, of the two kinds of devotees — those who worship Your personal form and those who worship Your impersonal form — who are better versed in Yoga?

Lord Krishna (to Arjuna): Those who worship My personal form with a fixed mind and with great faith in Me are considered by Me to be the most perfect in Yoga. But those who worship My unmanifest and impersonal form also attain Me.

However, worshiping My impersonal nature is hard since it is difficult to be perceived by a devotee.

But for those who worship My personal form, devoting all of their efforts to Me, acknowledging Me as the supreme being, and meditating on Me with single-minded devotion, I quickly become the deliverer out of the ocean of deaths and rebirths.

Therefore, fix your mind on Me alone. If, however, you are not able to fix your mind upon Me steadily, O Arjuna, seek to attain Me through the practice of constantly bringing the focus back to Me. If you are unable to do even this, work for Me by dedicating all your actions to Me. If you are unable to do even this, then renounce the results of all work.

Knowledge (Jnana Yoga) is superior to the practice of mind-control. Meditation on Me (Dhyana Yoga) is superior to knowledge, as one cannot meditate upon Me perfectly without knowing Me. Renunciation of the rewards of actions (Karma Yoga) is superior to meditation, as only a person perfected in meditation can renounce the results of his actions. Liberation and peace immediately follow renunciation.

One who does not hate anyone, is friendly and compassionate, does not consider himself to be the owner of anything, is free from ego, is forgiving, is always content, is always striving to reach Me with determination, and is self-controlled — he, being a true devotee of Mine, is dear to Me. One who is free from the emotions of joy, sorrow, fear, anxiety, honor, dishonor, and material attachment, and is always composed, even-minded, and full of devotion, is dear to Me. One who has no desires, is pure, is unconcerned about the results of his actions, and has no material motives, is dear to Me.

But one who pursues the teachings declared by Me in this divine song of Mine is the dearest to Me.

Key Takeaways

1. Krishna can be worshipped in both personal and impersonal forms. However, it is much easier and logical to worship His personal form. It is difficult for us, as humans, to perceive and love something that has no physical form. And this is not even needed.

2. Knowledge of the soul and the Supreme Soul (Jnana Yoga) is the first stage of Yoga. Then comes meditation on the Lord (Dhyana Yoga). Then comes the dedication of all actions to the Lord (Karma Yoga). And finally comes pure loving devotion to the Lord (Bhakti Yoga). Bhakti Yoga is the ultimate stage of Yoga. All these stages are necessary for a Yogi to pursue in order to reach Krishna.

3. The Bhagavad Gita is the ultimate guide for all seekers. One who seeks Krishna following its teachings certainly attains Him.

Chapter 13 - The Nature and the Soul

Arjuna (to Lord Krishna): O Krishna, I wish to learn about '*Prakriti*' (material nature), the 'Supreme Soul,' the 'field,' the 'knower of the field,' 'knowledge,' and the 'object of knowledge.'

Lord Krishna (to Arjuna): This body, O Arjuna, is called the 'field,' and one who knows the truth of it is called 'knower of the field.' I am the knower of the field present in all the fields. Knowledge of the field and the knower of the field is 'knowledge.'

Humility, unpretentiousness, non-injury, tolerance, sincerity, service of the spiritual master, cleanliness, steadfastness, self-control, indifference to the sense-objects, absence of ego, perception of the evils of birth, death, old age, disease, and the resulting sorrow, mental detachment with family and home, constant even-mindedness on the attainment of the desirable as well as the undesirable results, unalloyed devotion unto Me, solitude, knowledge of the soul, contemplation on the goal of true knowledge — all this is 'knowledge,' and all else is 'ignorance.'

I will now speak about that Supreme Brahman who should be understood and after understanding whom one attains immortality through liberation.

That object of knowledge has hands, feet, eyes, heads, mouths, and ears everywhere, and covers everything. Though it exists outside as well as inside all beings and objects, it is incomprehensible due to being very subtle. It is everywhere and in everything. Though actually undivided, that Supreme Soul appears as if divided in all beings as individual souls. That Supreme One is the light even of the lights, and beyond the darkness of ignorance. That is the knowledge, the object of knowledge, to be reached through knowledge. That is Me.

Material nature, being a tiny fragment of My divine nature, is the cause of all causes and effects in this world. And the individual nature one inherits from My material nature is the cause of all his experiences in life. Contact with the specific attributes of nature and the resulting karma decides the nature of the next birth of a soul.

Some see the Supreme Soul in the individual soul through Dhyana Yoga, some through Jnana Yoga, and some through Karma Yoga. Others, however, not knowing this, simply worship Me through Bhakti Yoga, hearing about My glories from wise sages. All of these Yogis transcend death by attaining liberation.

When one realizes that all kinds of beings actually exist in One Supreme God and spreads forth from there by assuming various forms of living beings, like humans, animals, fishes, birds, plants, insects, and so on, he attains My nature. As the one sun illuminates this whole world, similarly I illuminate the whole material body by giving it life.

Key Takeaways

1. Only knowledge about the soul, the Supreme Soul, material nature, and the various traits needed for the attainment of liberation are worthy of being called 'knowledge.' Everything else is ignorance. Such knowledge is essential for attaining liberation.
2. Krishna exists everywhere and in everything in a very subtle form. Therefore, it is difficult to perceive Him in that form.
3. Krishna's material nature is the cause of all causes in this material world.
4. When a soul enters this world in a body and comes into contact with material nature, it acquires certain positive and negative traits of nature, based on its previous karma. The way it uses these traits in its current life determines the form it will acquire in its next life.
5. The followers of all kinds of Yoga reach the same goal — oneness with Krishna.

Chapter 14 - The Three Modes of Material Nature

Lord Krishna (to Arjuna): Brahma, the god of creation, is the great womb in which I lay the seed of creation, and he is the one who brings it to fruition on My behalf. In a sense, the great Brahma is the mother, and I am the seed-giving father, O Arjuna.

Sattva (the mode of purity), *Rajas* (the mode of passion), *Tamas* (the mode of darkness) — these three *Gunas* (attributes) born of *Prakriti* (material nature) bind the soul in the body.

Of these three modes of material nature, the mode of purity, being immaculate, is illuminating and harmless, as it does not cause sin. It, however, binds the soul to the material world through attachment to material happiness and knowledge.

The mode of passion is of the nature of ecstasy born of lust and attachment to sense-objects. It binds the soul to the material world through attachment to the actions performed with the aim of sense gratification.

The mode of darkness is born of ignorance, which deludes all beings. It binds the soul to the material world through heedlessness, laziness, and sleep.

All these three modes of material nature fight for dominance over one's mind. Knowledge is a sign that the mode of purity has increased predominantly in one's mind. Greed, activity, restlessness, and hankering arise when the mode of passion becomes predominant. Absence of wisdom, inactivity, heedlessness, and delusion arise when the mode of darkness becomes predominant.

When one dies while the mode of purity is predominant in his mind and body, then he ascends to the heavenly planets of the learned sages. After dying in the predominant mode of passion, one is reborn on the earthly planets among those who are attached to material action. When one dies in the predominant mode of darkness, one is reborn in the wombs of the ignorant, such as animals and other creatures, and may also go to hellish planets.

The result of an action performed in the mode of purity is pure. An action performed in the mode of passion results in sorrow. An action performed in the mode of darkness results in even more ignorance.

A Yogi is aware that the three modes of material nature are the real performers of actions. Once the soul transcends these three modes of material nature, from which the body originates, it is freed from birth, death, old age, and the resulting sorrows, and attains immortality through liberation.

Arjuna (to Lord Krishna): What signs, O Lord, indicate that one has transcended these three modes of material nature?

Lord Krishna (to Arjuna): Such a person neither hates knowledge, activity, and delusion (the respective characteristics of the three modes of material nature) when these are present, nor longs for these when these are absent. He is indifferent to and is not disturbed by these modes of material nature. He remains firm in both sorrow and happiness. He is aware of his nature as a soul. To him, a lump of earth, stone, and gold are all the same. He is the same in honor and dishonor. He is equally on the side of a friend and of a foe. He is free of all material desires.

And one who serves Me, without swerving, through Bhakti Yoga, he automatically transcends the modes of material nature and qualifies to become one with Me through liberation.

Key Takeaways

1. Krishna is the creator of Brahma, and Brahma creates the universe on Krishna's behalf, using the material nature of Krishna.

2. *Sattva* (the mode of purity), *Rajas* (the mode of passion), *Tamas* (the mode of darkness) are the three *Gunas* (attributes) born of *Prakriti* (material nature) which bind the soul in the body.

3. The mode of purity is characterized by knowledge, the mode of passion by greed-motivated action, and the mode of darkness by ignorance and delusion.

4. All these three modes of material nature fight for dominance over one's mind.

5. When one dies in the mode of purity, he ascends to the heavenly planets. By dying in the mode of passion, one is reborn on the earthly planets. When one dies in the mode of darkness, one is reborn in the hellish planets.

6. Once the soul transcends these three modes of material nature, it attains liberation.

7. This material world is upheld by these three modes of material nature. A true Yogi is well aware of this fact and is thus equally situated in all situations. He is always focused on attaining Krishna through devotion.

Chapter 15 - The Supreme Person

Lord Krishna (to Arjuna): Free from pride and delusion, having conquered the evil of material attachment, absorbed constantly in self-knowledge, free from material desires, free from dualities such as happiness and sorrow — the undeluded persons attain the imperishable state of liberation.

Neither the sun illuminates My supreme abode, nor the moon, nor fire, but it is self-illuminated. After reaching there, the liberated souls do not return to this mundane material world.

I am the Supreme Soul, and the eternal individual soul dwelling in the living beings is just a fragment of Mine. I rule over all the senses as well as the minds of the living beings. Therefore, I am the ultimate enjoyer. The deluded cannot see Me as the soul dwelling in the material body, departing from the material body, enjoying through the senses and the mind, or associating with the modes of material nature. But the Yogis who have the eyes of knowledge can see Me doing all these activities.

I maintain the living beings by My energy and nourish all the plants as well. I am the source of light of the sun and the moon. I am the source of memory, knowledge, as well as the cause of their loss. I am the one to be known through the study of the Vedas. I am, in fact, the compiler of Vedanta (Upanishads) and the knower of the Vedas.

There are two kinds of persons in this world — the perishable and the imperishable. All spiritually unconscious beings are perishable, whereas those situated in the consciousness of My nature are imperishable. I am transcendental to the perishable, and even higher than the imperishable. Therefore, I am the Supreme Person.

Whoever knows Me as the Supreme Person knows everything, and worships Me wholeheartedly.

O Arjuna, this is the most secret science regarding the Supreme Person. Whoever comprehends this is regarded as wise and his duties are considered fulfilled.

Key Takeaways

1. Reaching Krishna's divine abode is the sole purpose of human life.
2. Krishna is the Supreme Soul, and all beings emerge from Him as tiny individual souls.

3. Krishna is the creator, sustainer, and destroyer of the entire cosmos, including all living things. He is the giver of all knowledge, memory, and intelligence, as well as the taker of them.
4. It is critical to acknowledge Krishna as the Supreme God. One who recognizes this is wise, whereas one who does not recognize this is deluded.

Chapter 16 - Divine and Demonic Natures

Lord Krishna (to Arjuna): There are two kinds of created beings in this world — the divine and the demonic. The divine attributes lead to liberation, while the demonic attributes lead to bondage.

Fearlessness, purity of heart, knowledge, steadfastness in meditation, charity, control over the senses, the performance of religious sacrifices, the study of the holy scriptures, austerity, straightforwardness, non-injury to the innocent, truthfulness, absence of anger, renunciation, peacefulness, aversion to slander, kindness, absence of greed, gentleness, modesty, absence of restlessness, vigor, forgiveness, fortitude, purity, absence of hatred, absence of conceit — these qualities belong to one who is born to attain divine nature, O Arjuna.

Pride, arrogance, conceit, anger, harshness, and ignorance — these attributes belong to one who is born to attain demonic nature. People of demonic nature do not know what is to be done and what is not to be done. They are devoid of purity, good conduct, and truthfulness. They believe the universe is a fabrication with no moral foundation.

They do not believe in God. They believe that the universe was formed by a strong longing for union with the opposite sex, rather than by a methodical causal sequence.

Such ruined beings of little intelligence engage in violent and destructive behaviors that are injurious to the world. Due to delusion, they continue to engage in lustful conduct and harbor wicked ideas. Being completely absorbed in worldly and bodily cares and concerns that have a transient influence, they wrongly assume that satisfying one's desires is the highest goal in life and that this is all there is to life. With such immoral intentions, they strive to accumulate wealth through dishonest means for physical pleasures.

They think, "This object of desire has been gained by me today; this I shall gain tomorrow. This is already there with me, and this wealth shall also be mine in the future. That enemy has been killed by me already; I shall kill others too. I am the lord; I am the enjoyer; I am perfect, powerful, happy, rich, and well-born. Who else is there like me? I will perform sacrifices to please the gods and demand from them the fulfillment of my wants. I will do charity for the same goal. I will rejoice all my life." Thus, such demonic people remain deluded by ignorance and ultimately sink into hell. Because of ego, power, arrogance, lust, and anger, these malicious people hate Me.

In their coming lives, I hurl these demonic people into the demonic wombs. Being born in demonic species birth after birth, these fools do not attain Me and keep entering even lower species.

This self-destructive gate of hell is of three kinds — lust, anger, and greed. Therefore, one should abandon these three immediately and forever. One who is free from these three gates to darkness strives for the betterment of the soul. Thus, he attains the supreme goal of liberation from the painful material world and gains My association.

He who ignores the regulations of the scriptures and acts under the impulse of lust, neither attains perfection, nor happiness, nor the supreme goal. Therefore, the scriptures are your guide in determining what should be done and what should not be done. You should act in this world in line with the regulations laid out in the scriptures.

Key Takeaways

1. There are two kinds of beings in this world — the divine and the demonic.
2. The divine beings possess pure qualities, and the demonic beings possess impure traits that are motivated by lust and ego.
3. Divine attributes lead to liberation. Demonic attributes lead to spiritual degradation into lower species.

4. Lust, anger, and greed are the three primary gates to hell. Therefore, one should abandon these three immediately and forever.

5. One should always follow the injunctions of the revealed scriptures instead of falling victim to lust and ego. Scriptures carry the secrets to happiness and fulfillment.

Chapter 17 - The Three Kinds of Faith

Arjuna (to Lord Krishna): What is the state of those who disregard the regulations of the scriptures and perform sacrifices with faith, O Krishna? Is it in the mode of purity, or of passion, or of ignorance?

Lord Krishna (to Arjuna): A human is defined by his faith, O Arjuna. The faith of each being is in accordance with his nature. Thus, faith is of three kinds.

Those in the mode of purity worship the demigods, those in the mode of passion worship nature-spirits and ogres, and those in the mode of darkness worship the ghosts and spirits.

Those who undergo severe austerities not authorized in the scriptures, motivated by ostentation, ego, lust, and attachment, senselessly torturing their own bodies and minds, as well as Me situated within the body in the form of the soul, are of demonic nature.

Also, the food, sacrifice, austerity, and charity preferable to each person are of three kinds.

Foods that improve life span, purity, strength, health, happiness, and affection, as well as those that are succulent, oleaginous, durable, and pleasing, are dear to those in the mode of purity. Those in the mode of passion crave bitter, sour, salty, extremely hot, pungent, dry, and scorching foods, which cause sadness, grief, and disease. Foods that are not properly cooked, insipid, putrid, and stale, as well as leftovers from other people's meals and impure food, are dear to those in the mode of darkness.

The sacrifice offered by those who are devoid of desire for the reward in return, and who perform it as a duty, in line with the scriptural regulations, is in the mode of purity. The sacrifice made for the sake of reward and ostentation is in the mode of passion. The sacrifice performed without scriptural regulations, without distribution of the food offered in sacrifice, without chanting of Vedic hymns, without offerings to the priests, and without faith in Me, is in the mode of darkness.

Worship of the demigods, the Brahmins, the spiritual masters, and the wise, purity, straightforwardness, celibacy, and non-injury to the innocent beings, are the "austerity of the body." Speech that is not agitating, and is truthful, pleasant, and beneficial, and the practice of the oral study of the scriptures, are the "austerity of speech." Mental tranquility, gentleness, silence, self-control, purity of nature, are the "austerity of the mind."

This threefold austerity practiced with faith by men devoid of desire for rewards of such practice is in the mode of purity. The austerity which is practiced for gaining good reception, honor, and worship, and with ostentation, is in the mode of passion, and its effects are unstable and fleeting. That austerity which is practiced out of foolish intent of torture of oneself or destruction of others is in the mode of darkness.

The gift which is given as a righteous duty, without an expectation of return, at a proper place and time, to a worthy person, is in the mode of purity. The gift which is given with the aim of getting something in return, or desiring some reward, and is given reluctantly, is in the mode of passion. The gift which is given at an improper place and time, to unworthy persons, and without respect, is in the mode of darkness.

'*Om* (the Supreme) - *Tat* (the Absolute) - *Sat* (the True, the Good, the Auspicious)' — this is My threefold designation. By that were created the Brahmins, the Vedas, and the sacrificial rites.

Therefore, the performances of sacrifice, charity, and austerity always begin with the utterance of "*om*" by My devotees, as prescribed in the scriptural regulations. Yogis conduct deeds of sacrifice, austerity, and charity by uttering *"tat"* without expecting rewards. The word *"sat"* is used in the sense of truth, goodness, and an auspicious act. Steadfastness in and actions meant for sacrifice, austerity, and charity, are also called *sat*. Whatever is offered in sacrifice, given in charity, and practiced as austerity, without faith, is said to be *asat* (false — the opposite of *sat*, truth), O Arjuna. It is of no use in this life or after this life.

Key Takeaways

1. The faith of a person is the best indicator of his nature.
2. It is foolish to believe that all forms of austerity are spiritually beneficial.
3. One should ensure that the food he eats, the penances he performs, the sacrifices he makes, and the charity he gives, are all of pure nature and in accordance with scriptural injunctions.
4. All spiritual activities should be free from material desire, ego, and impurity, and should be performed with pure faith in Krishna and a desire for His association.
5. One should know Krishna as "Om-Tat-Sat," meaning "the Supreme," "the Absolute," and "the Truth, the Good, and the Auspicious."

Chapter 18 - Renunciation and Liberation

Arjuna (to Lord Krishna): O Krishna, I wish to know the essence of *sannyasa* and *tyaga*.

Lord Krishna (to Arjuna): *Sannyasa* (renounced order of life) is the giving up of activities pursued with the expectation of positive outcomes. The giving up of the rewards of all activities is *tyaga* (renunciation).

Acts of sacrifice, charity, and austerity should never be given up. These three activities must always be performed, as they purify even the wisest of people. Even so, these actions should be carried out abandoning the desire for rewards.

The renunciation of obligatory actions by the ones who are yet to attain perfection in life is not justifiable. The renunciation of actions because of delusion is in the mode of darkness. He who renounces duty out of the fear of bodily discomfort performs renunciation in the mode of passion and does not reap the benefits of renunciation. When obligatory action is performed merely as a duty, O

Arjuna, renouncing the desire for reward, that renunciation is in the mode of purity.

It is not possible for the living beings to renounce actions entirely, but he who renounces the rewards of actions is called a man of renunciation. The threefold results of actions — evil, good, and mixed — accrue after death to those who are not renounced, but never to the *sannyasins* (the ones who follow a renounced order of life).

The five causes of the accomplishments of all actions are the body, the so-called doer, the various kinds of instruments (sense organs, mind, intelligence), the distinct functions of the organs, and the presiding deity of the respective sense organs. These five are the causes of any action, whether good or bad, a man takes with his body, speech, or mind. Thus, anyone who sees himself alone as the performer is of perverted intelligence and does not see things as they are. But the one who truly sees does not become bound by his actions.

Knowledge, the object of knowledge, and the knower form the threefold impetus to action. The instruments of action (the senses), the activity, and the performer of action are the three constituents of action.

Knowledge, action, the performer of action, intelligence, fortitude, and happiness are of three kinds each, according to the three distinctions of the modes of material nature.

Knowledge in the mode of purity is that by which one sees the same undivided Supreme Soul in all the separated individual souls. Knowledge in the mode of passion is that which perceives distinct entities in all beings. That trivial knowledge that is illogically and falsely bound to the body, as if it were everything, is in the mode of darkness.

That action which is undertaken as a duty and is free from attachment to itself or its rewards is in the mode of purity. That action which is performed by one who longs for the fulfillment of his desires, or with ego, or with too much strain, is in the mode of passion. That action which is undertaken out of delusion, without consideration of the potential harm and one's own ability, is in the mode of darkness.

The so-called performer of action who is free from attachment, non-egoistic, firm, enthusiastic toward the fulfillment of his duties in the manner approved in the scriptures, and unperturbed by success and failure, is in the mode of purity. The performer who is attached, hankering for the reward of action, greedy, of damaging mindset, impure, and subject to joy and sorrow, is in the mode of passion. The performer who is unsteady, materialistic, stubborn, unscrupulous, malicious, lazy, morose, and procrastinating, is in the mode of darkness.

That intelligence which understands what should be done, what should not be done, fear and fearlessness, bondage and liberation, O Arjuna, is in the mode of purity. That intelligence by which one wrongly understands righteousness and unrighteousness, and what should be done and what should not be done, is in the mode of passion. That intelligence which perceives righteousness and unrighteousness, and all other things, in a perverted way, is in the mode of darkness.

The fortitude constantly held through Yoga of meditation, by which one controls the mind, breath, and senses, is in the mode of purity. The fortitude by which one holds on to actions, lust, and wealth, longing for their rewards, is in the mode of passion. The fortitude by which an unintelligent person holds on to illusion, fear, grief, despondency, and conceit, is in the mode of darkness.

Happiness in the mode of purity is that which seems like poison at first, but proves to be nectar at the end, and is born of the goodness of one's intelligence. Happiness in the mode of passion is that which seems like nectar at first, but proves to be poison at the end, and is born through the contact of the senses-organs with the sense-objects. Happiness in the mode of darkness is that which deludes one, and is born of sleep, laziness, and heedlessness.

There is no being on this earth, or among the demigods in heaven, who is completely free of the three modes of material nature.

O Arjuna, the duties of the four classes of men — the Brahmins (the religious scholars), the Kshatriyas (the royal warriors and protectors), the Vaishyas (the merchants), and the Shudras (the laborers) — are assigned based on the attributes they acquire from material nature.

The duties of Brahmins include mental tranquility, self-control, austerity, purity, forgiveness, straightforwardness, knowledge, self-realization, and faith in Me. The duties of Kshatriyas are valor, splendor, firmness, skillfulness, not fleeing from battle, generosity, and lordliness. The duties of Vaishyas are agriculture, cattle-rearing, and trading. And the duty of Shudras is to provide service.

Each man achieves perfection by being devoted to his own duty and to Me.

It is preferable to do one's own duty properly, even if it is devoid of quality, than to do the duty of others well. One can avoid sin by fulfilling the obligations imposed by one's own material nature. Thus, one should never abandon his own duty.

Absorbed in a fully purified intellect, regulating oneself by firmness, renouncing sense-objects, dwelling in solitude, eating lightly, having speech, body, and mind under control, being ever-absorbed in Dhyana Yoga, having abandoned ego, power, pride, lust, anger, and accumulation of material possessions, being freed from the notion of ownership, and thus peaceful, one becomes fit for oneness with Me.

The perfected one, being blissfully one with Me, neither grieves nor desires, perceives all equally, and earns utmost attachment to Me, knows Me in essence — what and who I am — because of his devotion. Then, knowing Me, he attains Me immediately. Although being always engaged in all kinds of activities, the perfected one, taking shelter in Me, attains the eternal state of liberation by My grace.

Keep your consciousness always fixed on Me by mentally renouncing all actions and considering Me as the supreme. By doing so, you will overcome all obstacles by My grace and will eventually reach Me. But if you do not listen to My instructions because of your false ego, you will perish in your spiritual endeavors.

If you decide not to fight because your ego has convinced you that you are the doer, your decision will be in vain, for your material nature will compel you anyway.

Abandoning all forms of unnecessary engagements, take refuge in Me alone. By My grace, you will attain the supreme peace of liberation and the eternal abode of Mine. I will cleanse you of all your sins. Do not grieve.

All this knowledge that I have imparted to you is the highest secret. You should never teach this to one who is not austere, who is not a devotee, who does not serve Me, and who criticizes Me. He who would impart this supreme secret of Mine to My devotees with utmost devotion to Me, as revealed by Me in this divine song, will come to Me without a doubt. Spreading this wisdom is the highest form of service I can receive, and no one is dearer to Me than he who does so.

The sacrifice of knowledge that comes with studying this scripture is itself a service to Me. And whoever hears this conversation of ours with faith and without contempt is also liberated from the material world and comes to Me.

Have you listened intently to everything I have told you, O Arjuna? Has your ignorance-based delusion been dispelled?

Arjuna (to Lord Krishna): O Krishna, my delusion is destroyed, and my memory of my true identity is now restored through Your grace. I am firmly situated, and my doubts are gone. I will now act according to Your word.

Sanjaya (to Dhritarashtra): Thus, I have heard this wonderful dialogue between Krishna and Arjuna, which makes my hair stand on end with joy. O King, reliving this magnificent and sacred discussion, again and again, amazes and delights me.

Where there is Krishna, the Lord of Yoga, and where there is a disciple like Arjuna, there will certainly be prosperity, victory, power, and firm policy.

Key Takeaways

1. True renunciation is the giving up of the outcomes of all actions rather than the activities themselves.
2. Sacrifice, charity, and austerity should never be abandoned; rather, they should be carried out as a responsibility, with no hope of rewards, as with all other activities. Acting without regard for the outcome does not tie one to this world.
3. It is foolish to think of oneself as the sole performer of actions.
4. One who sees Krishna in all beings possesses pure knowledge.
5. Each person ought to engage in his own duty rather than someone else's.
6. The knowledge shared by Krishna in the Bhagavad Gita is the highest form of knowledge. This knowledge is only meant to be

received by the pure-minded souls. Studying this scripture with a pure mind dispels all delusions, and following its instructions leads one to Krishna.

7. One needs a surrendering and devoted mindset like Arjuna to benefit from the study of the Bhagavad Gita.

The Bhagavad Gita in a Nutshell

One's true identity

1. All beings are actually eternal souls. All are
    born, live, die, and are born again. This cycle
    continues until one attains liberation from it.
    One must always remain conscious of the fact
    of being a soul and being a part of the Supreme
    Soul, Krishna.

2. All beings forget their true nature and Krishna
    when they are born, and they become trapped
    in their various likes and dislikes. Such
    dualities bind beings to the material world. But
    those whose effects of karma have been
    negated by rewards or punishments through
    multiple lifetimes, become enlightened again
    about their spiritual truths and attain
    liberation through loving devotion to Krishna.

Krishna - The Supreme God

3. Lord Krishna is the Supreme eternal being.
    Still, he incarnates in various forms and at
    various times to restore righteousness in this
    world.

4. Krishna is the creator, maintainer, and destroyer of the entire universe, including all living things, and is present in everything and everyone.

5. Krishna is also found in all demigods and is the ultimate beneficiary of all sacrifices.

6. Krishna is everything and pervades the entire universe. Everything and everyone exist in Krishna. And a tiny fraction of Krishna exists in every person in the form of a soul.

7. One should never think of Krishna as an ordinary god. He is the Supreme One and is above all.

8. Being outside the dimensions of time, Lord Krishna is unborn and eternal. And who understands this is wise.

9. Lord's glories and opulence are immeasurable and are not possible for us, as humans, to comprehend. We can only understand a tiny fraction of His divine nature.

10. Lord Krishna is the source of all human emotions and traits. Krishna is the giver of all knowledge, memory, and intelligence, as well as the taker of them.

11. Krishna exists everywhere and in everything in a very subtle form. Therefore, it is difficult to perceive Him in that form.

12. One should know Krishna as "Om-Tat-Sat," meaning "the Supreme," "the Absolute," and "the Truth, the Good, and the Auspicious."

The universal form of Krishna

13. The universal form of Krishna encompasses everything that exists.

14. Human eyes are incapable of seeing Krishna in His universal form. Even gods and demons do not have the privilege of seeing that form.

15. Krishna's universal form is all-wonderful, all-brilliant, and unlimited.

16. Even the gods who are otherwise highly regarded by humans can be seen inside Krishna's colossal form.

17. Krishna's universal form, though divine, is terribly dreadful to view for us as humans. Among all else, the beholder can see in that form awful deaths unfolding that can easily terrify a human mind. That is why it is much easier for us to worship the Lord in His all-attractive, beautiful, and serene form as Krishna.

The purpose of human life

18. Reaching Krishna's divine abode is the sole purpose of human life.

19. One who reaches Krishna's abode never returns to the material world. This is the goal of human life.

20. Rare is the person who is able to see past the illusory nature of this material world, perceives Krishna as the Supreme Being, and pursues Him as his supreme goal.

21. The next life of a living being is decided by the prevalent state of his mind at the time of death. One can only reach Krishna if He remains prevalent in one's mind at the time of death.

22. A sincere Yogi who fails in his practice goes to heavenly planets after death, and thereafter is reborn in this world in conditions conducive to spiritual advancement. Thus, progressing through several lives, he ultimately reaches Krishna's abode to stay there forever.

Material nature

23. The material world is formed of Krishna's inferior material nature. Krishna's material nature is the cause of all causes in this material

world. However, His superior nature is also present here in all beings as souls.

24. When our senses come into contact with material nature, our minds are filled with a variety of sensory perceptions. Such fleeting sense experiences never bother an enlightened person.

25. *Sattva* (the mode of purity), *Rajas* (the mode of passion), *Tamas* (the mode of darkness) are the three *Gunas* (attributes) born of *Prakriti* (material nature) which bind the soul in the body.

26. The mode of purity is characterized by knowledge, the mode of passion by greed-oriented action, and the mode of darkness by ignorance and delusion.

27. All these three modes of material nature fight for dominance over one's mind.

28. When one dies in the mode of purity, he ascends to the heavenly planets. By dying in the mode of passion, one is reborn on the earthly planets. When one dies in the mode of darkness, one is reborn in the hellish planets.

29. This material world is upheld by these three modes of material nature. A true Yogi is well aware of this fact and is thus equally situated in

all situations. He is always focused on attaining Krishna through devotion.

30. When a soul enters this world in a body and comes into contact with material nature, it acquires certain positive and negative traits of nature, based on its previous karma. The way it uses these traits in its current life determines the form it will acquire in its next life.

31. Once the soul transcends these three modes of material nature, it attains liberation.

Qualities to develop and avoid

32. Ego never pays off and leads to one's downfall.

33. One of the most significant roadblocks to spiritual growth is a desire for sensual pleasures. It is essential to stay free of material desires and unattached to sense-objects at all times. Rather, one should concentrate on Krishna and cultivate a desire to reach Him.

34. A wise and even-minded person, knowing that all beings are pure spirit souls, views all beings with an equal eye. Free from dualities, a Yogi is neither excited by positive outcomes nor disappointed by negative outcomes. He always remains the same.

35. There are two kinds of beings in this world —
the divine and the demonic. The divine beings
possess pure qualities, and the demonic beings
possess impure traits that are motivated by lust
and ego. Divine attributes lead to liberation.
Demonic attributes lead to spiritual
degradation into lower species.

36. Lust, anger, and greed are the three primary
gates to hell. Therefore, one should abandon
these three immediately and forever.

Reaching the Supreme through Yoga

37. Knowledge of the soul and the Supreme Soul
(Jnana Yoga) is the first stage of Yoga. Then
comes meditation on the Lord (Dhyana Yoga).
Then comes the dedication of all actions to the
Lord (Karma Yoga). And finally comes pure
loving devotion to the Lord (Bhakti Yoga).
Bhakti Yoga is the ultimate stage of Yoga. All
these stages are necessary for a Yogi to pursue
in order to reach Krishna.

Jnana Yoga (Yoga of knowledge)

38. Right knowledge is crucial for a Yogi.

39. Only knowledge about the soul, the Supreme
Soul, material nature, and the various traits
needed for the attainment of liberation are

worthy of being called "knowledge." Everything else is ignorance.

40. It is critical to acknowledge Krishna as the Supreme God and see Him in all beings. One who recognizes this is wise, whereas one who does not recognize this is deluded.

41. Being unaware of spiritual realities causes one to become unnecessarily anxious.

42. A Yogi should ideally approach a wise sage and obtain divine knowledge under his guidance.

Dhyana Yoga (Yoga of meditation)

43. A man of knowledge constantly meditates on Krishna, which opens for him the doors to divine bliss.

44. A Yogi should sit firm in a quiet spot, with a focused mind, and practice Dhyana Yoga — the Yoga of meditation on the soul and the Supreme Soul, Krishna.

45. A Yogi must be moderate in his habits of eating, sleeping, and recreation. He should also be careful not to overstress his body or mind, as this will make it unsuited for Dhyana Yoga.

Karma Yoga (Yoga of action)

46. Karma is material action, and the effects of such action bind living beings to this miserable material world. The qualities of one's actions (karma) determine the quality of his next birth. A man of knowledge is not bound by such reactions of karma and attains Krishna after leaving the body. One needs to transcend these effects of karma to attain Krishna.

47. It is never advisable to avoid performing one's obligatory duties, as this results in sin. One should always strive to perform his duties well.

48. The outcome is never in one's control, so one should never be concerned about it. Instead, one should concentrate on doing his work efficiently.

49. One should dedicate all actions and their outcomes to Krishna.

50. Material nature is the real doer. One should never, out of ego, consider oneself to be the principal performer and controller of one's activities and outcomes.

51. A man of knowledge performs actions just for survival, not to accumulate wealth and possessions.

52. Sacrifice, charity, and austerity should never be abandoned; rather, they should be carried out as a responsibility, with no hope of rewards, as with all other activities. Acting without regard for the outcome does not tie one to this world.

53. Each person ought to engage in his own duty rather than someone else's.

Bhakti Yoga (Yoga of devotion)

54. One who is always engaged in the devotion of Krishna can attain Him easily. Devotion to Krishna purifies a person of all sins and leads him to godhood.

55. One need not offer riches to Krishna. Krishna accepts the simplest of offerings made by His devotees with a pure heart and loving devotion.

56. Lord's devotees take pleasure in worshipping Him, chanting His holy names, and discussing His greatness and pastimes. Such devotees are the most fortunate ones among humans. They are always eager to learn more about Krishna.

57. In the present age, devotion to Krishna is a must in order to know and reach Him.

58. Krishna can be worshipped in both personal and impersonal forms. However, it is much easier and logical to worship His personal

form. It is difficult for us, as humans, to perceive and love something that has no physical form. And this is not even required.

Spiritual activities and sacrifices

59. Various kinds of sacrifices are prescribed that cleanse one's karma and purify one's mind, making one fit for liberation.

60. It is foolish to believe that all forms of austerity are spiritually beneficial.

61. One should ensure that the food he eats, the penances he performs, the sacrifices he makes, and the charity he gives are all of pure nature and in accordance with scriptural injunctions.

62. All spiritual activities should be free from material desire, ego, and impurity, and should be performed with pure faith in Krishna and a desire for His association.

63. One should always follow the injunctions of the revealed scriptures instead of falling victim to lust and ego. Scriptures carry the secrets to happiness and fulfillment.

Renunciation

64. Giving up one's responsibilities is not the same as renunciation. True renunciation is

disinterest toward objects of pleasure, the rewards for one's actions, and negative emotions such as fear and anger.

65. Actions performed with such renunciation and dedicated to Krishna do not bind one to this material world and provides true peace.

66. True renunciation is the giving up of the outcomes of all actions rather than the activities themselves.

The demigods

67. The deluded beings worship the demigods, oblivious to the fact that Krishna is the Supreme God. The benefits people obtain from worshiping the other gods are temporary. Those who worship Krishna, on the other hand, attain Him and are blessed with His everlasting companionship.

68. The devotees of the other gods also worship Krishna indirectly. But this is not the recommended way of worshipping Him.

69. Krishna is the creator of Brahma, and Brahma creates the universe on Krishna's behalf, using the material nature of Krishna.

How the universe works

70. All worlds, including the worlds of gods, are subject to creation and annihilation. The material worlds manifest at the arrival of Brahma's day and annihilate at the arrival of Brahma's night. Brahma's one day and one night last for a thousand ages each. But Krishna's divine abode is transcendental to this cycle and is eternal.

Doubts

71. Doubts are hindrances to spiritual advancement, and one should get rid of them as quickly as possible.

72. Cynics who are more interested in spotting flaws than improving their knowledge can never achieve true wisdom.

73. Cynics and doubters, not realizing His supreme nature, always regard Krishna as an ordinary person or god.

The significance of the Bhagavad Gita

74. The knowledge imparted by Lord Krishna in the Bhagavad Gita is the oldest knowledge intended for humankind, having been given by Him at the inception of the universe. This establishes Krishna as the Supreme God and

the Bhagavad Gita as the repository of supreme knowledge.

75. The Bhagavad Gita is the ultimate guide for all seekers. One who seeks Krishna following its teachings certainly attains Him.

76. The knowledge shared by Krishna in the Bhagavad Gita is the highest form of knowledge. This knowledge is only meant to be received by the pure-minded souls. Studying this scripture with a pure mind dispels all delusions, and following its instructions leads one to Krishna.

77. One needs a surrendering and devoted mindset like Arjuna's to benefit from the study of the Bhagavad Gita.

Conclusion

The Bhagavad Gita is regarded as the sacred culmination of all Vedic wisdom. In other words, it is a condensed version of the tremendous amount of knowledge contained within the pages of large volumes of Vedic scriptures. It condenses all of that knowledge into just 701 verses, and even those have been summarized in this book for you.

In this concluding chapter, I would just like to urge you to not stop here.

No matter how hard we try to ignore it, we are all anxious, just like Arjuna. If you can see Arjuna within yourself, you can simply place yourself in Arjuna's shoes and speak with God through the Bhagavad Gita. When I want to talk to Krishna, I simply read a few verses from the Bhagavad Gita, and you can do the same.

This abridged version is designed to provide you a quick overview of the Bhagavad Gita and to aid you in your revisions without overwhelming you.

I strongly advise you to read the Bhagavad Gita's original verses in order to appreciate fully the purity and bliss of the conversation between the ideal devotee and the Supreme Lord. If you have made it this far and understand the value of studying this divine text, why not read the Bhagavad Gita as it was spoken by the Lord at least once?

The verses of the Bhagavad Gita are like nectar. And no matter how hard one tries to simplify its teachings, the person who reads God's words as they were uttered by Him will always gain the most benefit.

Lord Krishna, after enlightening Arjuna, says the following in the Bhagavad Gita: "And he who will study this sacred conversation of ours, I shall have been worshipped by him (through this study) by the sacrifice of gaining knowledge; such is My opinion." [BG 18.70]

Arjuna, after hearing the glorious song of God, exclaims, "O Achyuta (Krishna), my delusion is destroyed, and my memory (about one's true identity) has been regained by me through Your grace. I am firmly situated; my doubts are gone. I will now act according to Your word." [BG 18.73]

And Sanjaya, after witnessing the sacred conversation between Arjuna and the Lord, tells Dhritarashtra, "Thus, I have heard this wonderful dialogue between Vasudeva (Krishna) and the great-souled Partha (Arjuna), which causes the hair on the body to stand on end with joy." [BG 18.74]

Such is the effect of reading or hearing this sacred text.

As I mentioned in the Introduction, I refer to the Bhagavad Gita as "the end of self-help." After reading the Bhagavad Gita for so many years, I can confidently state that understanding all of its teachings will render all of the self-help books available to you useless. It offers all the guidance you may possibly require in order to live a happy and successful life.

The Bhagavad Gita is nothing but Lord Krishna Himself manifested as a book. No matter how you choose to study this scripture, remember to put all negative emotions, like ego and lust, at bay. What is needed is a complete surrender to Krishna, just as Arjuna did. Let Krishna be your spiritual master and guide. Let Him help you cross over this temporary ocean of material existence. Recognize Him as the Supreme Soul, of which you are just a fragment. Meditate on Him, and through devotion, fall in love with Him.

Follow Krishna's instructions and you will experience divine bliss. Finally, allow Krishna to liberate you and provide you shelter in His divine abode. May Krishna bless all!

About the Author

Hari Chetan is a spiritual and consciousness coach and has an immense amount of experience in the fields of religion, spirituality, theology, and ancient and modern philosophy. He is an expert in all major religions and spiritual philosophies including Christianity, Hinduism, Islam, Buddhism, Sikhism, Jainism, Judaism, Stoicism, Zen, Taoism, and Baha'i. However, Vedic philosophy is his primary area of interest.

Having discovered the oldest and the most confidential spiritual wisdom contained in the Vedic scriptures, Hari is on a mission to spread this knowledge to all corners of the globe. His goal is to awaken the entire world to the true identity of the self and God, and make everyone aware of the purpose of their existence, as this is the only lasting solution to all our problems. He currently lives in Kolkata, India with his family.

Connect with Hari Chetan:

harichetan.com
hari@harichetan.com
facebook.com/HariChetanOfficial

A Gift for You

In the daily commotion that characterizes our lives nowadays, it is quite easy to lose track of oneself. And so it is important for us to maintain our mental equilibrium by connecting with our spiritual selves on a regular basis.

Download Hari Chetan's **free Bhagavad Gita Workbook** designed especially for the readers of his books.

This workbook will help you test your knowledge of the core concepts given in the Bhagavad Gita, and to keep you on track in your spiritual journey.

Try it. It's free to download and is very useful!

Visit **www.harichetan.com** to download.

The Bhagavad Gita Series

Book 1: Bhagavad Gita - The Perfect Philosophy: 15 Reasons That Make the Song of God the Most Scientific Ideology

Book 2: Bhagavad Gita (in English): The Authentic English Translation for Accurate and Unbiased Understanding

Book 3: 30 Days to Understanding the Bhagavad Gita: A Complete, Simple, and Step-by-Step Guide to the Million-Year-Old Confidential Knowledge

Book 4: The Bhagavad Gita Summarized and Simplified: A Comprehensive and Easy-to-Read Summary of the Divine Song of God

Book 5: Mind Management through the Bhagavad Gita: Master your Mindset in 21 Days and Discover Unlimited Happiness and Success

All Books: Bhagavad Gita (In English) – The Complete Collection: 5-Books-in-1

Made in the USA
Middletown, DE
16 August 2023

36858897R00087